Learning to Write as a Hostile Act for Latino Students

COUNTERPOINTS

Studies in the Postmodern Theory of Education

Joe L. Kincheloe and Shirley R. Steinberg
General Editors

Vol. 257

PETER LANG
New York • Washington, D.C./Baltimore • Bern
Frankfurt am Main • Berlin • Brussels • Vienna • Oxford

RAUL E. YBARRA

Learning to Write as a Hostile Act for Latino Students

PETER LANG
New York • Washington, D.C./Baltimore • Bern
Frankfurt am Main • Berlin • Brussels • Vienna • Oxford

Library of Congress Cataloging-in-Publication Data

Ybarra, Raul E.
Learning to write as a hostile act for Latino students / Raul E. Ybarra.
p. cm. — (Counterpoints; v. 257)
Includes bibliographical references (p.) and index.
1. English language—Rhetoric—Study and teaching—United States.
2. English language—Composition and exercises—
Study and teaching—United States. 3. Report writing—Study and
teaching—United States. 4. Hispanic Americans—Education—Language arts.
5. Hispanic Americans—Language. I. Title.
II. Series: Counterpoints (New York, N.Y.); v. 257.
PE1405.U6Y38 808'.042'0712—dc22 2003025254
ISBN 0-8204-6824-X
ISSN 1058-1634

Bibliographic information published by **Die Deutsche Bibliothek**.
Die Deutsche Bibliothek lists this publication in the "Deutsche Nationalbibliografie"; detailed bibliographic data is available on the Internet at http://dnb.ddb.de/.

Cover design by Lisa Barfield
Cover art by Augustine Romero

275 Seventh Avenue, 28th Floor, New York, NY 10001
www.peterlangusa.com

TABLE OF CONTENTS

ACKNOWLEDGMENTS

Because this book project grew out of numerous discussions with colleagues and staff at the University of Massachusetts in Boston, I would like to extend my gratitude to all those faculty and staff in the many departments, in particular to the faculty and staff in the College of Public and Community Service, for their support and nurturing community. A big thank you as well to the faculty and staff in the Latino Studies Program and the Gastón Institute at the University of Massachusetts Boston for their commitment to producing research that contributes to the development of the Latino community.

I personally want to thank Donaldo Macedo in the Applied Linguistic Graduate Program whose own discourse and praxis on how we can improve the education of Latinas and Latinos in the United States has inspired my ideas for this book. In addition, I want to extend a personal thank you to four students who put up with my stressful moments during the entire process in writing and editing this book, and who provided me with a backboard for which to bounce ideas and an avenue for which to vent my frustrations, Diana Zegarra, (the Latino Studies Administrative Assistant) Maria Luisa Plasencia, and Maria Moreno, Anna Frader (all students in the Latino Studies Program). I would also like to thank the staff at Peter Lang Publishing, and Bernadette Shade in particular, for their professionalism and support of this book project.

Finally, I would also like to express my sincere gratitude and my indebtedness to two very dear friends and colleagues, Professor Nancy López in the Sociology Department at The University of New Mexico in Albuquerque who has always been supportive of my work and Augustine Romero, a sculptor and painter, for granting permission to use the art on the cover.

Raul Ybarra

TRANSCRIPTION CONVENTIONS

SYMBOL	**DESCRIPTION**
/?/	Inaudible language
/ /	Words difficult to comprehend and are questionable
{ }	Additional information has been added that is not part of the transcription
...	Words have been deleted
—	Interruption or sudden shift in topic
____	Name of person has been deleted

ABBREVIATIONS

BW	Basic Writing
CSU	California State University
ESL	English as a Second Language
GPA	Grade Point Average
GRE	Graduate Record Exam
LARES	Latino American Recruitment Educational Services
UIC	The University of Illinois at Chicago

CHAPTER 1

My Story—As Example

> Arguments exist that state "authenticity" or "authentic voice" can never truly be reached because realities are socially constructed. Individuals might experience an epiphany and see themselves in the context of a new reality, but in truth that reality is constructed to manipulate the individual. I take the position that when Xicanas(os) understand that manipulation and alienation exist, this realization becomes a stepping–stone to experiencing the process of conscientization. It needs to be clear that conscientization is not a goal one reaches and then one is done. Conscientization…is a process of reflection and action that is ongoing.
>
> —Margis Bertha Ávila, 2002, p.1

My Story

For most of my life, I lived in California agricultural towns—Livingston, Merced, Atwater, Fresno—until a few years ago when, to work on my doctorate, I traveled to Chicago. I was reared, in a small farming community in the San Joaquin Valley where the majority of the work is seasonal fieldwork and the majority of the working people are migrants of Mexican descent. Every year between June and September my family migrated north to Oregon and Washington to harvest the crops: apples, pears, cherries, peaches, plums, and all kinds of berries. This began when I was four and I traveled with my family until my fifteenth year. We lived in tents, cars, and in migrant camps. Many times, we lived with two or three other families in small houses and apartments. We would return late in the summer to California, just in time to harvest the grapes and almonds. Then during the fall and winter months, we stayed in Livingston while my father worked for a local farmer. This is where my siblings and I went to school.

Although my summers were spent in a community that was mostly Mexican, eight months out of the year I was in schools dominated mostly by Anglos. Because of school, my language shifted from primarily Spanish to mostly English. My friends went from primarily Mexican to mostly Anglo. However, this shift was not a quick or easy transition. There were times when

I was embarrassed at home because of my family's way of life. We lived in a house with no running water. Our bathroom was an outhouse. We took our baths in a big washtub. I was embarrassed by my first language, Spanish; I was embarrassed by the foods that we ate, mostly beans and tortillas; I was embarrassed by the clothes I wore, the usually baggy clothes passed down to me from my older brother. School was not much easier to deal with either. I was embarrassed because of my skin color. I was embarrassed in my many struggles learning to speak, read, and write English.

From the moment I started kindergarten, school had been a struggle. In kindergarten, I was held back because I couldn't speak English. In elementary school, other children would make fun of my accent and name. In high school, I would get into fights because students would call me "wetback" or "wet," "greaser" or "spic." If these incidents, and many others, were meant to discourage me from my continuing to go to school it did not work. In fact, it had the opposite effect. I put in extra effort to correct the problems I had with English. After each incident, I concentrated more on school and on my schoolwork. Early on, I practiced English as much as I could, whenever I could. I practiced speaking and reading aloud to lose my accent. I read whatever I could get my hands on and practiced writing and spelling. During the period between the 1960s and 1970s, the school I went to was tracked. From what I remember, there were four tracks in all: A, B, C, and special education. During my elementary years and throughout most of my middle school years, I was always put in the C track.

One reason why I was put in this track was that I always had problems with writing. In elementary school, when a written assignment was returned to me, what I mostly remember seeing were the many red marks on my papers pointing out my errors: spelling errors, tense errors, punctuation errors, handwriting errors. Being marked down for handwriting errors in my written assignments has become particularity interesting to me now, because as I saw more and more errors being marked in my papers, my handwriting became worse. By the time I was in sixth grade, I had lost my motivation to write. In its place, I developed strategies to avoid writing whenever I could. I would miss school; I would conveniently get sick so that I would be sent to the school nurse, and sometimes even home; I would not turn in assignments (or turn them in late). Of course, none of these strategies worked and I still ended up writing the assignment. During my eighth–grade year, I was moved out of C track into A track, except in English where I still struggled. Although I can't recall what skills I learned in taking A and B track courses (because I was already behind in all the classes many of the teachers gave me worksheets to fill out) I did learn another ineffective strategy to avoid writing even more in English class. My handwriting went from bad to worse.

In high school, I was put back in the lower track for all of my classes, except now they were called remedial courses (I was put in remedial courses for my four years of high school in subjects like history, math, and English). My freshman, sophomore, and junior years in high school were almost replicas of each other, both in terms of the classes and the instructors. We did almost the same type of work and had the same type of assignments. The only thing I remember doing in any of those courses, including English, was mostly worksheet–type exercises: fill in the blank, true/false, multiple choice, and definition. When I did have to write, however, I wrote the minimum. I just figured the less I wrote, the fewer mistakes I would have. In English, we occasionally had a long paper to write, usually a research paper, but these assignments were actually some of the easiest because I didn't have to (necessarily) write the paper. All I had to do was copy the passages I needed from my sources to my paper. Then I would change some of the words to make the different passages fit better.

Halfway through my junior year in high school, I realized that I was out of place. I did not seem to fit in with the majority of the school's population. Most of the student population by this time was either white or recent Mexican immigrants. There had been an in–surge of migrants from Mexico over the past few years, making school more difficult for those of us, a small group, born and reared in the United States. Not only were the white students looking at me suspiciously; but so were the recent immigrants from Mexico. To white students, I was not white; to Mexican students, I was not Mexican. Not only were the white students telling me I did not belong, but many Mexican students told me as well. I had lost most of my Spanish (my primary language now being English) and I had never been to Mexico—many of them stating that I was brown on the outside, but on the inside I was white, a "coconut."

I decided, sometime during my junior year, that school was not leading me anywhere. Back then, I was not completely sure about why I dropped out. I know now that my dropping out had to do, in part, with being bored (as an institution, school was not interesting to me), with being fed up and feeling frustrated and alienated. I was also angry at most of the teachers because they didn't seem to care about my being at school. I was tired of being alone. I had no contact with any of my instructors outside regular classroom instruction. And I felt like a failure. I had no motivation; there was no one to encourage me and no one to push me. I didn't see myself finishing high school, let alone going to college. But I did not plan on quitting either. I just found myself not going to school.

One day I was needed at work an extra day—I worked at the local community center—so instead of attending school, I worked. The following day my father needed me at home to help with some remodeling he was doing to our house; so I stayed home to help. The next day I ran errands for my father and his friends. The next thing I knew, I had skipped a few days of school. Those few days quickly turned into a week, and I did not miss the classes. Actually, I was feeling more relieved then anything else. I felt calm. There was no pressure about having to turn in work; no pressure from the hostility I felt from teachers and students.

Then during my second week away from school, as I continued to help with the remodeling of our house, I saw a familiar ugly, yellow pickup truck in our drive way. I knew immediately who the person was. Only one person drove that truck, my shop teacher, Pirus Abraham. I don't remember hearing him knock—I think he just walked into the house. After he came into the house and saw what I was doing, he offered some pointers on how to do some of the remodeling. He even helped a little. He stayed for about two hours, talking to me as he helped. Somehow, during our conversation, he got me to commit to going to his office early the next morning, and I did. I didn't go to my classes that day though. I just talked to Mr. Abraham for a few hours and then I helped around the shop. Over the next few days, he showed me how to use much of the equipment in the shop—in the process, giving me tips on remodeling a house. He never pushed me to return to my classes. In fact, I don't remember him bringing up the subject of returning to school at all.

It was not until years later while doing research for this book that I discovered one very important reason why Mr. Abraham played such a positive and important role in my life—as other instructors had done later in my life. An important part of the student's integration into school is the interaction that takes place between student and faculty. This is what I did not have in school: interaction with an instructor to motivate me, encourage me, and push me.

By the third week after dropping out, I was back at school, sitting in my old classes. However, there was a difference in my attitude. I wanted to be there, not necessarily in the classes, but I wanted to go to the shop area where Mr. Abraham taught. Every chance I could, I would go to the shop, and I would spend my free time there, before school, during lunchtime, and after school.

Another important event took place that year—my junior year in high school. My father decided not to migrate north to follow the harvesting of crops. For the first time since I could remember, I was actually at home at the end of the school year and not on the road. And even though the school year ended, I still kept going to the shop class on a regular basis. I would drop by in the mornings before work and come back right after. When school started in the fall, I returned to high school for my last year. At the start of my senior year in high school, I found out that I had fulfilled most of my required courses for graduation, which included English, writing courses, math, and science. However, I still had to take one more history course, but other than that, I could take whatever elective course I wanted. With Mr. Abraham's help, I became an office assistant for the main office: I ran the school switchboard, ran errands for the principal and the dean of students, and I kept the "calendar of events" up to date. During the mornings, I found myself constantly in contact with many teachers and administrators. I became so motivated that I wanted to sign up for two shop courses because I was finished with school by lunchtime. However, my adviser recommended that I not sign up for more classes. Instead, he advised me to put more time at work in order to help my family. So I did. Right after lunch, I walked over to the Livingston Community Center where I worked as a janitor, making the minimum wage, about $2.35 an hour. I had started working there during the early part of my junior year and continued working there throughout the summer after my graduation.

Nothing eventful happened my senior year. I was still bored with school and I still didn't talk to many people. Yet I wanted to be there. The only class I had any homework in was history, but that work wasn't very difficult. This particular history course was geared for those students who had difficulty passing history. Most of the assignments involved worksheets and I was good at filling those out. I didn't miss a single day of classes that year.

That year I had not planned to go on to college. In fact, I don't even remember thinking about college. I didn't go to any of the meetings the high school arranged for those students applying to college (or to talk with college representatives or get help filling out applications for financial aid). I don't even remember getting any notices about such meetings. I do know that my parents wanted me to work full time when I finished high school to help them out financially because I was the oldest male living at home; my older brother had moved out. I do know that my high school adviser recommended that I not go to college, but to continue helping out my family. I was probably more surprised than any one of my friends or family members that I did go on to college. I decided to go to college when I saw my Anglo friends preparing to leave at the end of summer. Some had already left; others were eagerly talking about going to college. I felt left out. I too wanted to go to college. Moreover, I could not see myself working for $2.35 for the rest of my life. So when the start of the semester came around, I decided to visit the local community college in Merced, California. I had no idea what I needed to do to register or what I needed to take with me.

When I arrived at the community college, someone in the registrar's office told me that I needed to take placement tests for reading, writing, and math, and one was being offered that day. So I scrambled for paper and pen. After the placement test, I met with an adviser who explained the results and advised me about what courses to take. Here I was—I hadn't even visited a college before—the first day of the semester, going through a process I had never gone through before, totally confused, tired, and frustrated listening to someone telling me I had to take basic courses in math and writing. But, I was not discouraged.

In September of 1975, I began college at Merced Community College. At eight o'clock Monday morning, the first day of the fall semester, I started my very first college class, Basic Writing, as I had started most of my high school writing courses. I figured that there was not that much difference from those students in my high school courses. I sat in the back of the room, with no paper or pencil, waiting for the class to begin, looking around and watching everyone else take out their pens or pencils and their notebooks. I didn't know it at the time, but this was to be my most difficult course.

During the second day of class, as soon as we received our first writing assignment, a diagnostic writing, I realized I was in trouble. I don't recall what the topic was, but I do know we had ten minutes to write a paragraph. The problem was that I didn't have any idea what belonged in a paragraph. I had never learned to write one, so I wrote some sentences that looked more like a list than an essay. In this class, besides continuing to do worksheets (with formats like multiple choice, true/false, and fill in the blank) there was a bit more emphasis on writing paragraphs. I learned that in a paragraph we had to include a topic sentence, at least three supporting sentences, and then a transitional sentence. We would take examples of good paragraphs (paragraphs that demonstrated this beginning, middle, and end structure) from a book or worksheet and modeled them as we created our own. This was the extent of our writing. By the end of the semester, I was writing paragraphs. I could also identify the subject, verb, and predicate in each of my sentences. However, even though I progressed to the point where I knew what a preposition was, to pass the course I still had to write an entire essay.

The problem was that I didn't know how to write an essay. I wrote on the exam what we did throughout the course. I wrote a paragraph. I made sure it had the three parts that I needed: a beginning, middle, and an end; my topic sentence; my three supporting sentences; and my concluding sentence. The essay wasn't very long, but I had written extra large so that it at least appeared to be a page. I didn't understand why I failed and no one bothered to explain to me why I failed. Instead of taking this course again, immediately, as was recommended, I took other courses. I thought that the more exposure I had to writing before I took Basic Writing again, the more I would understand about writing. Eventually, I thought, when I did retake the course I would know more about how to write, thus ensuring my passing. The problem was that I not only avoided taking the Basic Writing course, but I avoided taking any course that required much writing because I was embarrassed that I didn't know how to write and fearful that I was going to fail not only English courses, but any course that required much writing.

In the spring of 1978, after two and a half years of taking classes at Merced Community College, I transferred to California State University (CSU) Fresno. At first, going to Fresno didn't seem to be too difficult. However, there were many things to take care of and not enough time. For the first time I had to get an apartment by myself, take care of the electricity, telephone, cleaning deposit, car payment, and food. Then came buying books and materials, studying, working—I wasn't prepared for any of this. I also realized that I had already completed four years of college and was close to graduation, but I still had not retaken the Basic Writing class or any other writing course (this included the required composition course, the research–oriented composition course, and the advanced writing course). All were required for graduation.

I stopped taking classes after the spring semester of 1979. I used the excuse that I had run out of money to justify my quitting. However, my decision to leave college at this time was quite different from when I dropped out in high school. At this point in my educational career, I did not fit the traditional definition of a dropout, "a permanent withdrawer," because I had every intention of returning to college as soon as I figured out what I wanted to do with my life.

Between 1979 and 1982, I worked in a variety of jobs. I worked as a chicken farmer, janitor, teacher's aide, and finally as a substitute teacher (this was my last job before returning to college). In fact, I had held a long–term substitute position (over a year and a half) as a PE teacher at Livingston Middle School in my hometown. It was this job more than any other that had the biggest influence on my returning to school. Through this position, I began to form friendships with other teachers. I also contacted those teachers who had helped me when I was in high school like Mr. Abraham, and I also found myself working more and more with Latino students who had problems in school; they had problems like high absenteeism, low motivation, and constantly getting in trouble with teachers. These were all students who reminded me of myself. I found that I enjoyed working with these students. I liked the fact that other teachers would come to me for advice on these students.

In the fall of 1982, as I continued to be a long–term substitute teacher at Livingston, I enrolled again at Merced Community College on a part–time basis for the purpose of retaking the Basic Writing course and eventually going on to CSU Fresno to get my teaching credentials. I thought completing my Basic Writing requirement would be easier and definitely less expensive at Merced. However, before I could register for the Basic Writing course, once again, I had to take a placement test.

There was really nothing out of the ordinary about the placement test. Placed in rows, alternating seats from each other, we were given an exam booklet and two No. 2 pencils. We were given exactly thirty minutes to write an essay, but we couldn't start writing until the person proctoring said it was time. He first had to read the prescribed, prewritten directions, and then he looked at his watch for what seem to be a very long time before he uttered the word "go." As we wrote, student assistants walked up and down the aisles. They made sure we weren't cheating; they answered questions; they replaced pencils for students. Exactly at the end of the thirty minutes, we were told to stop writing and the student assistants collected the essays. I felt that we had just gotten started.

The essays were read and evaluated later that afternoon, and the next morning one of the English instructors gave us the results. Based on my scores—which I never saw—it was recommended that I take the ESL (English as a Second Language) course, a writing course for non–native English speakers. But because I had already attended college and had over fifty–six credit hours, I was allowed to enter the Basic Writing course. Later, I found that because of the number of credit hours I had, I could actually have entered the required writing course, but I was not told about that by my adviser or instructor. In any case, what I did know was that my writing had gotten worse.

The first time I had taken Basic Writing we spent some of the class sessions working on punctuation exercises. Though we were tested on punctuation periodically, we mostly concentrated on writing paragraphs. This second time taking Basic Writing we followed the same procedure as before, except now I also had to enroll in the Writing Lab two hours a week for additional help.

In the Writing Lab, we first were given a diagnostic exam on punctuation, which was then analyzed for errors. Prerecorded cassette tapes and worksheets (all numbered), which covered our weak areas based on the results of the exam, were provided by the lab so that we could listen to the tapes and answer the worksheet questions. Wall dividers separated the booths from each other, and each booth had a cassette player built into the desk. The headphones were numbered (engraved) and assigned to us when we came into the lab during our scheduled visits. After we were finished with the tape and worksheet, we were given another pre–recorded audio cassette and another worksheet that covered another area of punctuation. This went on for the entire semester.

What upset me was that the worksheets weren't even looked at. When we were finished with a worksheet, we took our worksheet up to the person grading them, and all the grader did was place an answer sheet over our worksheet. Our marks were to correspond with the marks on the answer sheet. We had to get at least 80 percent of the answers correct to move to the next level (the next worksheet) or we would have to do that particular worksheet over again. I realized that this Writing Lab was not interested in helping me learn about writing, but learn about what I knew about writing, which was very little. At the end of the semester, to pass the Writing Lab all we had to do was demonstrate competence; to show competence we just needed to progress to a certain worksheet number.

As with the Writing Lab, there was no grade given for this course. We received either a Pass or a Fail. The coursework included some writing, but the majority of the time we sat in small groups and discussed the areas in which we were having trouble in our worksheets. The instructor would move from small group to small group and join in on the discussion. None of this work, however, counted toward passing the actual Basic Writing course. For that, we had to complete the coursework assigned, and as the previous Basic Writing course, I had to pass a written exit exam. Once again, for the exit exam we were to write a two–to three–page essay on a pre–selected topic. This topic I do remember because, never having thought about "What does the U.S. Flag mean to you" sounded unusual to me. Of course, it had the usual "Make sure you write a well–organized paper, outline, then proofread, and make sure to use plenty of details" rule. The exam took place a week prior to finals week so that the instructors could meet with the students and discuss our options—retake Basic Writing, or take the required composition course. After completing the exam, I knew I hadn't passed. I don't think I wrote more than half a page because I couldn't think about what to write about the flag. I remember I had this queasy feeling deep down, but I went to the conference because I thought that I had a slim chance of passing, and if I prayed hard enough, something would change. Of course, I didn't pass.

In the spring of 1983, frustrated and angry because I still had to pass the required writing course, I resigned from my long term substitute position and enrolled again at CSU Fresno on a full–time basis. I hoped to pass the Basic Writing course there so that I could complete my undergraduate work and then enter the education program for my teaching credentials. I was angry at the fact that the two Basic Writing courses I had taken did not count toward my degree. I was frustrated because I could not understand why I had failed the exit exam and I was scared of not passing the course a third time. I didn't know what I would do if I failed Basic Writing again. I was not getting any financial aid by this time so I was not under any college time limit to graduate. I felt I was just wasting time having to retake this course when I could have been taking more courses in my major. (At that time, my major was not English. Rather, it was Plant Science.) I did question whether passing this course was worth all the effort I was putting into it, but I continued.

Since I was not getting any concrete answers as to why I could not pass Basic Writing, I came to the conclusion that either there was something wrong with me or the university was trying to keep me from succeeding because of my cultural background and skin color. I was confused because I did not know what I needed to do. Worse yet, with each failure I became resigned to this confusion of not knowing why writing was so difficult for me. I could not understand why I did well in my other courses, but I was struggling with writing. Even more disheartening, I was struggling with *Basic* Writing. I became angry because neither reason made sense to me. I saw English instructors as uncaring or as racist. I continued because I wanted to know what was being kept from me. I did not realize at that time that I was going through a period of cultural adjustment.

The first two times taking Basic Writing my strategy was to learn, and in doing so I had hoped to pass. This time around, my goal now was not to learn, but to do whatever it took to pass. Previously I had kept quiet, speaking only when spoken to. This time I was determined to be more aggressive. I decided that I was going to ask the instructor questions about what was required in writing essays and about passing the exit exam. The previous Basic Writing classes concentrated on the parts of the essays, sentences or paragraphs. In this class, the focus was on writing and rewriting entire essays. The instructor allowed for a number of rewrites, so I took full advantage of this by taking each essay to her several times. My belief was that if I took her my essay enough times she would eventually find all my mistakes for me. I knew at times she became irritated with me because I took up a lot of her office time, but I did not care. I was determined to pass. In addition, in this class, we practiced writing timed essays every two weeks; this was an exercise that was not done in my previous two times in taking Basic Writing. I went from writing one paragraph at the beginning of the semester to writing several by the end.

There was still an exit exam required to complete the course, and as in the other Basic Writing courses I had taken, an in–class essay assignment written under a time limit of fifty minutes. This scared me because I knew I wouldn't be able to take my draft to my instructor for her to look at beforehand. I had also become comfortable writing two or three drafts before handing the paper to my instructor. What concerned me most of all, because of having previously failed two exit exams, was the possibility of failing again.

After taking the exit exam, I met with my instructor. She confided in me that she was disappointed with my timed essay. However, she felt strongly that my writing was much better than the exam had shown so she petitioned for me to enter the required composition course, showing samples of my writings to the director of composition. Both agreed that I could enter the regular composition course, provided that I also register with the Writing Center. Although I was ecstatic and relieved that I finally passed, I was still fearful, suspicious, and angry because I had passed only because of the instructor's help. I felt that she had written the essays for me, and I thought that she felt sorry for me and that is why she petitioned for me to pass. In actuality, I passed because of my own work, which convinced her I could write.

Still, I was happy to have finally passed. I had already made plans to go to the Writing Center anyway, so I happily agreed. However, what worried me was that I had two more writing courses to go. Furthermore, I still did not understand why I had so much difficulty with writing. I knew I still had problems. I just didn't know where or why. My suspicions were that my writing problems had something to do with me—that there was something wrong with me. Because of this fear and suspicion I delayed taking the required composition course. I was scared that the writing instructor would discover that I couldn't write. I justified my delaying taking the required writing course by convincing myself that I needed a break from writing.

I didn't take the required composition course until the spring of 1984 (two semesters after passing the Basic Writing course). By this time, I was very close to graduation. I had fulfilled all my courses in my major, Plant Science, and most of the university's required courses. The only two courses left were my writing courses. I enrolled in the Writing Center as suggested. I expected another struggle in passing this course; at the very least, I prepared to spend another year in college. But I was wrong. I only took one semester to complete the course.

In this writing class, we concentrated on four essays, all personally based topics. We could rewrite them as many times as we wanted and at the end of the semester, we put our final drafts in a portfolio and turned them in to our instructor. The only part I found difficult was that twice during the semester the instructor required that we pass out copies of our essays to the rest of the class so that other students could read them and comment. I volunteered quickly, if not first, to have my paper discussed so as to get that requirement out of the way. Interestingly, I found myself actually spending less time working on drafting than in the Basic Writing course, but I continued to talk to my instructor often. Mostly we spoke about the ideas I had and wanted to write about. She would listen to me and encourage me to write more. Even though I still struggled, I found that I could write, that I wanted to write, and I did very well in this course. I was excited and had not felt this excited about school since I had first entered kindergarten.

Because of what had happened in the past I was still very suspicious. I was not sure if I had learned how to write an essay or if my instructor was "taking it easy" on me. I suspected the latter, so when I registered for the research class (in the fall of 1984), I registered for her class again. This was my thinking. I needed to improve my GPA and thus, I needed an A. I had gotten an A from this one particular instructor once in the required writing course; therefore, I could do it again in the research class. I knew her teaching style and she knew my learning style. I found out early what her topics were going to be, all based on personal life experiences, and so I started writing the essays before the course actually started. This gave me even more time to write and rewrite. I continued talking to the instructor before and after class as well. I went to the library to do my research. I was also beginning to feel more hopeful. A surprising thing happened to me toward the middle of that semester. My instructor suggested that I consider entering graduate school in English. I was only one semester away from graduating—we had had previous conversations about my plans and I had told her I was not sure what I was going to do.

At first, I wasn't sure whether or not to take her suggestion seriously, because the struggle of my passing Basic Writing was still fresh in my mind. But she persisted. She constantly brought up my potential as a writer, my persistence at trying to understand a problem, my motivation and discipline as a worker—all the characteristics of a graduate student. At first, I was suspicious. I still had many problems with my writing, and there were still many things I did not understand about writing. For a while, I even thought that I was being set up to fail again.

By the end of the semester, I was seriously considering entering the graduate program in English. Not only was I getting A's on my written assignments, but other students were coming to me for help or advice. I did not know how to help. What I did was talk to them to find out what they wanted to write about and encourage them to write as much as they could about their topic then bring the paper back to me. I knew, though, that I was not much help because there was too much I needed to know. I still had one semester to complete my degree in Plant Science, so I took advantage of that semester by taking more English and writing courses—I took two advanced writing courses (a 200–and a 300–level course), an introductory creative writing course (lower division), and an American literature course (300 level). All together, I took four English courses.

I needed to prove to myself that I was capable of taking English courses and doing well in them. I did. I received A's in all of them. I felt more confident than ever before about knowing what I was doing, but I still struggled with writing. I continued to have problems with tenses, punctuation (in particular with the comma), and with spelling. I talked to my freshman composition instructor about these problems. She was the one who initially helped me to realize that maybe the problems I had with writing were not with me being intelligent enough, but more to do with my language and my culture. At that time, I was not aware that writing, learning, and culture are all connected, and that the structures of schools and classrooms represent and promote a culture that was foreign to me. I also did not know at that time that for many students of color, the most difficult part of the writing course was the exit exam. I graduated with a bachelor's degree in the spring of 1985, ten years after I graduated from high school. Later, I found that ten years to complete a degree was not uncommon for Latino students

In the fall of 1985, I entered the graduate program in English at CSU Fresno. I needed money, however, to pay my rent, buy my food, buy my books, and pay bills (this didn't even include the registration fees and tuition). I asked the chairperson if I could delay coming into the program for one semester while I worked. She told me to apply at the Writing Center as a tutor, and there I could work enough hours to live on.

I was hesitant at first. My first thought was, "Me—a tutor?" I knew that I did not know enough and I knew that the students I helped would ask me questions I would not know how to answer. But I needed the money, and all that was needed to become a tutor was to be a graduate student in English. For that, all I had to do was submit a writing sample and have someone in the department recommend me—she, the chairperson of the English department, agreed to give me a recommendation. There was only a two day training session I had to attend before I could begin tutoring. At the tutor training session, we were told that the focus was on peer tutoring. (We read books and articles by Peter Elbow on peer editing.) We were told that we were not to deal with grammar or punctuation; rather, we were to listen and talk to the students and encourage the students to write and rewrite. After tutoring a few times, I realized I had gone through this process before. These are the same techniques I used when writing my own papers. I had gone through this process when I was a student going to the Writing Center as part of my stipulation to get into the freshman composition course. I had gone through this in the composition course I had taken. Now, I was to encourage students to go through this in which process they brought their papers to me.

By my third semester, in the graduate program, the director of composition suggested and encouraged me to apply for a teaching position to teach freshman composition. Again, I felt the same lack of preparation as when I began tutoring. I didn't think I was prepared enough although I had completed a year in the master's program in English and a year as a tutor, but I applied anyway because the stipend to teach at the composition level was higher than what I was getting as a tutor. Because of my limited time in the field of English—my undergraduate work being in Plant Science—some members in the English department didn't think I was prepared to teach the freshman composition courses, so I was given a Basic Writing course to teach instead. This way I could get experience with teaching and writing before I was put into a regular composition course. I was not angry when this decision was made because I agreed with many members of the English department. I thought that the Basic Writing course was just that—*basic*—even though I had struggled through this course. It was the only writing course that I struggled through three times before passing. I saw teaching this course as an opportunity to learn not how to teach but how to write. I figured I would eventually learn enough about writing the so–called "correct English" to help my students feel comfortable about writing an academic paper.

While teaching the Basic Writing courses, however, I did notice a disturbing placement pattern in the various composition courses. While the majority of the students in Basic Writing classes were Latino (with a lesser percentage of African Americans and Asians), in the regular composition courses the students were mostly white. Here is where my initial questions and interest about Latino students and their struggles began. I wanted to know why such large numbers of Latino students were placed in Basic Writing. I completed my graduate program in three years (1988) and received my master's in English composition. However, I was still not satisfied that I had learned what I needed to learn about writing or about teaching writing, especially Basic Writing. I still needed and wanted to know why I struggled and why many other Latinos struggled with writing. I decided to pursue my graduate studies at the doctoral level. I applied to several universities across the country where I could continue to pursue my interest in writing and with Basic Writing.

In September 1988, I entered the doctoral program in English at the University of Illinois at Chicago (UIC), specializing in language, literacy, and rhetoric. I chose UIC not because of what I knew about the program (I knew very little), but because of the people I met and talked to. There was Professor David Joliffe, the director of Composition at UIC (currently a Professor of English at De Paul University). I told him that I wanted to teach Basic Writing. He was delighted with my choice because he had struggled to get people to teach Basic Writing. I met a graduate student, Juan Guerra, (currently a Professor of English at the University of Washington). He told me about his interest: the literacy practices of an immigrant Mexican family. He then introduced me to Professor Marcia Farr who was doing research, along with Professor Lucia Elias–Olivares, on the literacy practices of Mexican families in Pilson, Illinois.

When I entered the graduate program at UIC, I had not narrowed my interest yet, but I knew that it had to involve Latino cultures and Basic Writing. As I explained to Professor Farr in one of my many conversations with her, as teachers of Basic Writing, I felt that we do not know how to teach writing to Latinos or to many other minority students. I told her of the many struggles I had gone through in elementary school, high school, and college. I told her about my frustration, fears, and anger about taking writing, especially Basic Writing. I told her about how I saw many of the same fears and anger in many of my Latino students as I continued to teach Basic Writing. Professor Farr suggested that the problems I had and that many other Latinos struggled with were not just problems with learning to write. Rather, the problems had more to do with language, with family, and the culture of the students; that often these cultures were different from that of the school.

I thought about whether I had gone through a cultural transformation. I did not think I had at first, but as I stepped back and thought about who I was and where I was, I realized I had. When I first started kindergarten, I was held back because I could not speak English. In the third grade, I was almost held back again because I could not write very well. My father had a strong sense for keeping the hierarchal structure in the family. He already had one son in the second grade and did not want two sons in the same grade at the same time for fear that it would reflect badly on him. In junior high school and high school, I could not move beyond remedial classes in English. As I progressed through high school, I spoke with little or no Spanish accent when I spoke English, but I did have an accent when I spoke Spanish. I would switch from Spanish to English when I could not think of the word in Spanish. When I decided that I was going to do whatever I needed to do to pass Basic Writing, I passed. This was a crucial point in my cultural transformation. Since then, my grade point average went from a C average to an A average. I have received my bachelor's degree in Plant Science and a master's in English composition, both fields dominated by Anglos. Then I entered the Ph.D. program in English, a field of study that is predominantly Anglo.

Conclusion

While progressing through my doctoral program, I slowly defined my field of study. To help me in answering why writing is so difficult for Latino students and why do many Latinos fail to acquire the writing level expected of them even after twelve years of schooling during the course of my graduate studies, I particularly focused on writing and writing issues of color, in particular Latinos. I found that cultural and communication differences do play a part in how Latino students respond and react to being taught academic writing. Cultural differences contribute to the different and/or negative impressions Latino students have about writing and other English courses. As Farr (1986) states "aspects of one's culture are a part of the tacit knowledge that members of a particular group unconsciously share simply by virtue of being members" (p. 200): When the culture or ethnic backgrounds of the members differ, "meetings can be plagued by misunderstandings, mutual misrepresentations of events and misevaluations" (Gumperz and Gumperz, 1982, p. 2).

These misunderstandings and misevaluations ultimately have a negative effect on the student, which ultimately affect school achievement. Erickson (1996) supports this argument when he argues that the problem is that we know very little about how differences in language and differences in culture affect school achievement. Understanding where the students come from and what problems they are having is important when teaching writing because overcoming these problems are key components to these students (Latino students) completing college (Valverde, 1987). Understanding why Latinos do poorly in writing courses is becoming an ever–more important issue because Latinos are now the fastest growing minority group in the United States. These statistical realities of Latino student concerns warrant serious investigations. Indeed, the frequency of failure among Latino students in particular in Basic Writing courses suggest a (dis)connection—or dissonance—between the cultural backgrounds and corresponding thought processes of Latino students in the writing classroom.

To date, research in this area is virtually nonexistent. Understanding, and consequently overcoming, why there is a (dis)connection is key to reversing the low retention rate of Latinos in the United States. (Ybarra, 2001). Thus, this book shows how school helps in contributing to Latinos' poor performance in the classroom. Moreover, this book shows that cultural differences do contribute to the poor performance of Latino students and other minority students in composition classes at the college level. This book also provides a basis for evaluating communication patterns and communication breakdowns in a classroom setting. Each chapter in this book examines the mainstream assumptions of education and culturally relevant pedagogy and provides a basis for evaluating communication patterns and communication breakdowns in a classroom setting. This book also shows how communication breakdowns, because of cultural differences between Latino students and Anglo–mainstream instructors do contribute to the poor performance of Latino students and other minority students in composition classes at the college level.

Whereas I used my own personal experiences in this chapter (Chapter 1) as an example to show how I dealt with Basic Writing as both a student and instructor to better understand the Latino students in my classes, Chapter 2 examines the mainstream assumptions of education. Chapter 2 explores how Latino university students internalize, and eventually begin to verbalize, negative, distorted, and poorly informed mainstream perceptions concerning Latino identity. The focus is on the cultural schemata of academic discourse and why this is a difficult task for many minority students, in particular Latino students.

In Chapter 3, I focus on four Latino students in a Basic Writing class. This chapter shows how school helps in contributing to Latinos' poor performance in the classroom. Students who are not part of the mainstream, particularity Latino students, see this pattern of writing structure as confusing and view it as a hostile attempt to change who they are. In this chapter, I show how this does epistemological violence to Latino students of tracking because of the marginalization and cultural implications that takes place.

In my final chapter (Chapter 4), I explore the pedagogical implications of what I observed in a Basic Writing classroom, and patterns that fit those general patterns associated with the Anglo-mainstream group by comparing them to patterns that have been described in other classroom discourse studies. By comparing the demands that are embedded within mainstream language and literacy practices with those structuring influences found within the Latino culture, we can better understand where academic structure conflicts with the oral discourse patterns of Latino students, which will give us the insight we need to see how students from different ethnic groups and cultures respond.

CHAPTER 2

The Classroom Discourse Structure

> For some time folklorists have known that European folktales are organized around themes of three parts. We have "Goldilocks and the Three Bears"; if a character has to go through ordeals there are usually three of them; if a king has a daughter he has three, and they marry three brothers; and so on. We have only really just noticed recently that this organization is more than just folklore.
>
> —Scollon and Scollon, 1981, p.33

Introduction

The goal of this study, as with all studies that deal with different communicative patterns between cultures, is ultimately to help the student. Although the results of the study do not explain all the reasons for the disproportionately high dropout rates for Latino students, it does give us further insight into why some students reject school, why some Latino students continue to have problems with writing even after completing the freshman composition courses in college, and why some Latinos excel. Taking Basic Writing for many Latinos reinforces the idea that they are not good enough to enter the required composition course; that in order for them to become proficient in writing, they must give up their cultural identity. Others see this as a way to succeed, to get ahead.

Studying how writing courses affect Latino students differently is important because Latino students are entering college in record numbers. In contrast to the increasing number of Latino entering college, however, the number of Latino students completing college is still very low. Out of all Latinos who go on to college, nationwide only 25–30 percent complete their undergraduate education, and even then, for most, it takes six years or more to complete their undergraduate education (Porter, 1990). This is important because as Oscar Porter (1990) shows, while the dropout out rate for other cultural groups drops significantly after the first year, the dropout rate for Latinos stays consistently high every year.

Writing courses appear to be significant in determining whether the students will complete college, and these courses are increasingly becoming more important because at many of our colleges and universities, students are required to pass this course to complete college. Many colleges and universities use writing courses as a way to make sure all students entering the university or college write at a certain level. If students do not meet the level required, they are placed in remedial a course to "fix" the problem.

Not awarding college credit for Basic Writing further heightens the suspicions Latino students have about academic writing for these students must still take both the regular composition course and the research composition course. This practice is not uncommon. According to Linda Knopp (1995), "[o]nly one in five institutions awards degree credit for developmental classes" (p. 8). Similarly, at the University of Illinois at Chicago (UIC), being placed in a Basic Writing course means to many Latinos that they have to take three writing courses to fulfill their writing requirements.

As it stands now, all students at the University of Illinois must fulfill the writing requirement by completing two writing courses: English 150 is for limited–English speaking students and English 152 is for students who need extra help with writing. English 160 is the regular composition course and English 161 is the research course. Placement into English 150, 152, or 160 is based on the results of a test given to all entering freshmen. Those students who are placed in 150 or 152 must still take both English 160 and English 161. Since student placement statistics reveal that a disproportionate number of students placed in Basic Writing courses are Latino, Basic Writing classrooms were chosen as the sites for the study.

To understand how teaching writing affects non–mainstream students (specifically Latinos), we need to understand, describe, and analyze the culture of the classroom. Thus, the purpose of the chapter is to show how pedagogical assumptions and practices together with the communication patterns of Basic Writing instructors toward their Latino students affect writing performance. Moreover, because this chapter explores how Latino university students internalize, and eventually begin to verbalize, negative, distorted, and poorly informed mainstream perceptions concerning Latino identity, the focus is on the cultural schemata of academic discourse and why this is a difficult task for many minority students, in particular Latino students.

Overview of Basic Wring

The purpose of Basic Writing at the University of Illinois at Chicago, as stated by Downs et al. (1991) in the "Content Guidelines" for teaching Basic Writing, is not so much "to teach students how to write, but to help students understand how writing works in the world, especially the world of the university":

> Remember the goal is not to turn students into expert critics but rather to give them a sense of confidence by helping them realize that each piece of writing is produced by a human being for some purpose in the real world, a world of which they area part. (p. 5)

Thus, the focus of Basic Writing, though still a preparatory course, is not on skills, but rather on understanding the writing process as a whole, from the beginning stages of ideas to the final product. Instructors of Basic Writing at UIC are encouraged to assign their students a significant amount of reading and writing, drafting and revising (both in-class essays and out-of-class essays), and conferencing with students (Downs et al., 1991, pp. 4–9). By steering students through a series of revisions, the students will not only create their own models of writing, "but will learn academic discourse through using it" (Farr and Daniels, 1986, 81; Downs et al., 1991, p. 32).

The instructor, whom I shall call Pat, came to this course with the requisite background in composition teaching. Having taught college–level writing courses at two other urban institutions (De Paul and Loyola Universities), she was entering her second year teaching Basic Writing at UIC. She also held the reputation of being considered one of the better instructors in the program due to her energetic style of teaching and her propensity for encouraging lively discussions among her students. From such indicators, Pat appeared to be a successful instructor for Basic Writing students. I thus predicted that I would witness a positive impact of her pedagogical practices and interaction with her Latino students on their written performance.

The Syllabus

Instructors of Basic Writing at UIC are encouraged to assign their students a significant amount of reading and writing, drafting and revising (both in class essays and out of class essays), and hold conferences with students (Downs et al., 1991, pp. 4–9). By steering students through a series of revisions, the students will not only create their own models of writing, "but will learn academic discourse through using it" (Downs et al., 1991, p. 32; Farr and Daniels, 1986, p. 81). I begin with the class syllabus because, as Stock and Robinson (1989) argue, the syllabus serves as a base from which my analysis will emerge. Through the instructor's syllabus we can see the teacher's "beliefs about learning, as well as her political and ethical commitments" (p. 315). Through an examination of this one syllabus, I show how the teaching of writing and the presentation on how to write is organized according to a very specific model. I discuss how writing instructors not only expect students to demonstrate this model in their writing, but expect students to live this model.

The First Section of Syllabus

As required by the English department, the instructor begins the session by presenting a syllabus which outlines what she wants to accomplish for the entire term. (To view the syllabus in its entirety, see Appendix A, Syllabus.) In addition to reading her syllabus to the class, she also distributes the syllabus to her students and, as required, submits a copy to the Composition office (Downs et. al, 1991, p. 19).[1] This first section is the general introduction to the class. The instructor introduces herself (as Pat), the times she will be in her office for conferences, office location, and times and place the class would meet:

Syllabus	
UIC Fall 1991	Office Hours:
Instructor:	M 11:00–12:00
English 152	and 2:00–3:00
M,W,F 12:00–12:50	W 2:00–3:00
W 11:00–1:50	F 12:00–2:00

Because the instructor wanted and expected to confer with her students individually periodically throughout the semester, she wanted students to freely come to her office when they needed help. Thus, she lists the location of her office, along with times of her office hours, and phone number because she wanted to convey to her students "that they are genuinely welcome to talk to [her]" (Fraher, 1984, p. 120).

The next section of the syllabus begins with "Aims of the Course." Here, the instructor describes, in a general manner, her expectations of what she wants her students to accomplish:

- To develop clarity of thought by reading, thinking, rethinking, redrafting, revising, editing, and polishing prose;
- To organize and develop ideas in coherent writing;
- To become confident in writing academic discourse.

Pat's objective by the end of the semester is to get her students to write in academic discourse. Although Pat did not state this directly, the implication is made quite clear by her three stated goals: first—"To develop clarity of thought," meaning to write clearly, directly, and to avoid any "unnecessary complex prose" (Watkins and Dillingham, 1989, p. 5); second—"To organize and develop ideas," meaning to shape the ideas "to the larger intentions of the paper," organize and keep the paper coherent without sacrificing clarity (Watkins and Dillingham, 1989, p. 39) and finally—"to become confident in writing academic discourse," meaning to write in their academic voice. Through her three stated goals, Pat is suggesting to her students that if they do what she has asked, they should be well on their way to writing academic prose on their own. This is important because Pat is letting her students know that she is aware that the students must, in time, produce text that the academic community wants. As Bartholomae (1988b) writes, the student "has to do this as though he were easily and comfortably one with his audience, as though he were a member of the academy...." (p. 274).

To help the students become members of the academy Pat, will use the certain writing tools that she has listed: "reading, thinking, rethinking, redrafting, revising, editing, and polishing prose." By performing each task the students will thus eliminate unnecessary information, correct those features that are wrong, and expand on what is correct or accepted and also learn about how to organize and structure according to Western essayist literacy patterns. Moreover, the students will learn to become proficient in their critical thinking and use of language because they will have been allowed time "to appropriate (or be appropriated by) a specialized discourse" (Bartholomae, 1988a, p. 274). Pat herself has stressed this idea of appropriating a specialized language to her students in her lectures. She stressed to her students that they must start practicing how to use academic language early in the semester in one of her lectures to the class:[2]

> You can get rid of half that stuff and say what you want to say. Now, Letty does what a lot of you do, and in academic writing try not to do this, "In the ad I chose about the beer Michelob Light." I want you to focus on just telling it to me straight. A number of students in the other class say, "Well I'm going to write about" or "this is what I think about." Don't do it. Just tell me your thoughts. I'm going to tell you about my thought, "I love Alena's cough drop she just gave me." Don't tell me to tell you about my thought I love Alena's cough drops. Just say "I love Alena's cough drops." So you're up here, you're now authority. Even if you don't know anything. Act like the authority /?/. It's the mask that you got to put on. So what you're doing is just saying , "In the in the ad of Michelob Light." Don't say the ad I chose. What you chose doesn't make any difference. You're the authority on this ad. And you're going to tell, tear this ad apart. Okay?

When she says, "So you're up here, you're now authority. In academic writing, you act like authority. Even if you don't know anything," Pat is advising the students to take control of their own essays, to speak—at least pretend to speak—with authority as though they were the experts (Bartholomae, 1988a, p. 274). Pat wanted her students to practice being writing experts to "dare to speak it or to carry out the bluff, since speaking and writing will most certainly be required long before the skill is 'learned'" (Bartholomae, 1989a, p. 274). By trying, by participating, and by emulating, the students will in time produce the type of text that the academic community wants.

This idea is supported by scholars such as Pascarella (1980), Valverde (1987), and Tinto (1987). All three scholars show that an important part of the students' integration into college is the interaction that takes place between students and between students and the faculty. Each type of interaction—students interacting with other students and students interacting with instructors—play major roles in helping the student become a member of the school community. One affects the other. This student interaction, in turn, shows the students how to interact with faculty (Pascarella, 1980; Staton, 1990). Part of the interaction involves speaking and interpreting what is being spoken. This interaction is important because it helps people establish social and ethnic identities and group membership (Jepp et al., 1993; Cazden, 1986; Gumperz, 1982). For example, at the beginning of one class session Letty and Connie were talking about their calculus class—more specifically, about an exam they were preparing to take. Pat allowed the students to participate briefly in the conversation that Letty and Connie were having about calculus:

Connie: (whispers) Which chapter are you in?
Letty: Chapter 3; okay it's uh 3.6, 3.7, 3.1, 3.2, 3.3, 4.1, 4.2.
Connie: Chapter 3. We don't do Chapter 4 then?
Letty: Yeah. Chapter 4, 4.1, 4.2.
Connie: Oh.
Letty: Okay?

At this point in time, the instructor began her lecture for the day:

> Pat: We'll be doing sentence combining exercises, and I'll just give you the, the sheets before you leave. We'll just make sure however we break, however long we go. If you walk out with those, and I think that'll be self– explanatory. Then we'll see; we'll see how time goes. Where's /?/? What is it? Anybody's heard of /?/? Is she, she coming?

Instead of ending their conversation, however, Connie and Letty changed over to whispering, so for a few minutes the tape recorder couldn't pick up what they were saying. Then they raise their voices enough for the microphone to pick up once again, and because they raised their voices, other students could now hear them and joined in.

Letty: /?/. I like doing these things.
Connie: Yeah, I guess.
Letty: Honey, that's a long way. We probably won't even get to that.
Connie: {Laughs}.
Letty: {Laughs}.
Students: {Ask Connie and Letty what they are working on}.
Connie and Letty: (respond in unison) Calculus!
Letty: And we got to go quick. I mean no stopping in the washroom today.
Student: Do you have a test today?
Letty: Yeah. Everybody just goes for the test. The room gets so filled right away, and then you don't have any seats left.
Connie: There about 20 people there, and then when the test comes, its all filled up.
Letty: It's all. Whatever, about a 120 people there?
Student 1: 1–A?
Letty: Huh?
Student 2: 1–A?
Letty: No, it's—
Connie: 165.
Letty: Calculus 165.
Connie: It's business calculus.

Student 2: Oh.
Student 3: {Inaudible}.
Letty: I am freaking today (laughs).
Pat: (Laughs) What time is your exam? We'll give you time to get your—
Letty: It's at one.
Pat: At one o'clock?
Letty: Right after this class.
Pat: Right after this class (says it in unison with Letty). {Bell Rings for the class to begin}
Pat: We should let us out a little bit early, so you'd have a chance to–
Student 3: Yeah, that's a good idea.
Pat: (Laughs)
Letty: (Laughs)
Student 4: Some more of that.

Pat allowed for the discussion to continue for a few minutes, then at a certain point raised her voice to regain control of the class: "What I'd like to do this hour is work on structure…." Connie and Letty stopped their conversation as the focus of the topic shifted back to the lesson of the day, working on organizing and structuring an essay.

Pat, to get her students into the academic community, knows that the student "must speak and write…toward such familiarity" (Stock and Robinson, 1989, p. 318). Interaction is the key by which the students are going to learn about becoming members of the academic society. What better ways then to have the students interact with one another so as to practice? Although this is the type of interaction Pat wanted, the topic was unrelated to writing and somehow Pat had to end the discussion. As Shirley Brice Heath (1978) explains:

> Classroom language has overriding rules that reflect the teacher's authority to decide who speaks, on what topics, and for how long. Many teachers have a high regard for the conversational mode, yet the goals of instruction and learning prevent them from allowing uncontrolled classroom conversation. Thus they provide rules for discussion, class meetings, or lessons that prescribe for students the limits of their powers of decision making about such talk. (p. 6)

Before long, Pat interceded and refocused the conversation back to writing. By doing so Pat was letting the students know how she was guiding "classroom activities and modalities of social interaction" (Stock and Robinson, 1989, p. 314). As Hugh Mehan (1979) states, "It is incumbent upon the students to keep the special normative demands of the classroom separate and distinct from those of other situations when they engage in classroom interaction" (p. 196). Pat was balancing the interaction of the students with what she wants the students to learn so that the students might "form into a productive learning community" (Stock and Robinson, 1989, p. 314).

The Middle Section of the Syllabus

The instructor, in the middle section of her syllabus—what Pat entitles "The Conduct of the Course"—explains how she is going to go about getting the students to write in the expected manner. This section contains the class requirements: a listing of the texts to be used in the classroom; a short explanation of the attendance policy; as well as explanation of the reading and writing assignments. Located here is also a "Grading" section. In it Pat explains how at the end of the term she is the one who will evaluate/judge the students on how well they conform to her guidelines—essentially, how well they can demonstrate that they have become members of the academic community.

The Third Section of the Syllabus

The third and final section of the syllabus is a week–by–week description of what Pat plans for the entire fifteen–week semester (see Appendix A, Syllabus). This section is basically a listing of the course of study. Pat shows how the reading assignments are sequenced with the writing assignments, which in turn are sequenced with her class objectives:

PROPOSED SYLLABUS:

Week 1 Read "Customs" (247–251) and "American Men Don't Cry" (209–292)
Week 2 Read "Families" (85–89) and "Fitting In" (123–127). No class on Monday
Week 3 Read "Girlhood among Ghosts" (15–20) and "Halfway to Dick and Jane" (21–33)
Week 4 Read "Hair" (120–122), "Shooting an Elephant" (228–235), and "The Village of Ben Suc" (209–215)
Week 5 Writing #1 due
Week 6 Read "Custer Died for Your Sins" (331–334) and "Incident" (37)
Week 7 Read "When I was a Child" (47–54)
Week 8 Read "From Vietnam, 1979" (165–169)
Week 9 Read "Arrival at Manzanar" (158–164)
Week 10 Read "We Real Cool" (136)

Week 11 Writing #3 and #4 due
Week 12 Read "Graduation" (3–14) and "Alien Turf" (145–157)
Week 13 Read "I Learn What I Am" (139–144).
Week 14 Writing #5 due. No Class Friday, Nov. 29
Week 15 Writing #6: In–class essay

Separating "the course of study" into its own section is important because if students do not initially see how thoroughly the ideological assumptions are structured and integrated, a week by week description of the entire semester is provided. More importantly, Pat also shows how the reading assignments are sequenced with the writing assignments, which, in turn, are sequenced with her class objectives. This also allows students to see how each section of the syllabus can be distinctly identified, with all the sections connected to each other from beginning to end in a sequential and hierarchical organizational–type pattern (Mehan, 1979, pp. 35–74). This sequential and hierarchical pattern allows for the syllabus to stand on its own as a separate text—to be understood as a completed text even outside the confines of the classroom (Scollon and Scollon, 1981, p. 48).

This sequential and hierarchical pattern allowed me to see the class, for the entire semester, as a lesson composed by a set of rules—or a set of transactions. There is an introduction with a thesis statement that clearly states the argument and purpose of the class (the aims of the course); the body of the text which contains paragraphs supporting the stated purpose (the conduct of the course); and a conclusion that outlines the semester.

The Discourse Cultural Model

This pattern I have just mentioned can be described simply as a beginning, middle, and an end. Thus, the connection to the opening quote: "For sometime folklorists have known that European folktales are organized around themes of three parts" (Scollon and Scollon, 1981, p. 33). R. Scollon and S.B.Scollon also postulate that this three part pattern is a complex of theoretical and educational positions of viewing the world as a reality set (1981, p.41 and 50). They go on to say: "New and given information in essayist prose are signaled syntactically and lexically…and requires a higher attention to syntax and especially to sequential relations among sentences" (p. 48). These features make this style of discourse a distinctly identifiable register.[3]

Although, I do stress that it is not simple by any means, this, as Farr (1992), Heath (1983), and Scollon and Scollon (1981) argue, is a way of cognitively structuring and viewing the world around components of threes. Farr (1992) points out that this discourse pattern is not just limited to written discourse. Heath (1983) and, Hymes (1974), as well as Farr (1992, 1991, 1990) stress that this style of discourse is seen as a part of both speaking and writing. Patricia Stock and Jay Robinson (1989) put it this way:

> Writers and readers behave in much the same way as speakers and listeners do; that individuals who speak and hear, and write and read, for and with one another over a period of time in a given context to constitute…an interpretive community. (p. 319)

As Scollon and Scollon state: "Nothing outside the text is needed for interpretation" (1981, p. 48).This is supported by Farr (1992) when she writes:

> In other words, speaking and writing are alternate ways of using one's language capacities, or communicative competence, and very often both models are used within a single speech event or literacy event. (p. 8)

This concept is synthesized by Farr (1992):

- The text is direct and explicit in its direction, "cohesive and clearly bounded," an "isolable entity";
- The text fictionalizes the author and audience leading to a decontextualization of the written language from actual situations and an idealization of readers and writers as rational minds and of text as perfectly rational;
- An emphasis on the logical order internal to the text, with "attention to syntax and especially to internal relations among sentences," as well as a high percentage of new information. (pp. 8–9)

Class Lecture as Model

This discourse style is embedded in Pat's lectures. At the beginning of many of the class sessions, Pat either outlined, verbally or wrote out on the chalkboard, what she wanted to accomplish for that particular day, often referring to her syllabus to confirm that she was on schedule. If there were any changes to this course of study, the instructor lets her students know about the changes. For example, in the following passage taken from a class session during week three, the instructor states:

> Before, even before you even think about how you're going say it you need to start thinking about what is it that I'm going to say. So today I want to start just thinking a little bit about audience, and then we'll talk about the academic audience, and then we'll work on your papers. Okay. Let's just look at these—and see how much time it'll take you to write this out and hand them in to me. (Counts softly) One, two, three. Remember on the syllabus I said that I would ask you to do in–class writing and that would count for part of your grade but I wouldn't grade it. This is the kind of thing where I go through, and I check off that you completed this assignment. I don't grade it, but you get credit for it in writing. That's what this is saying. For this assignment, I'm reading from this paper, you will be writing two descriptions of the city or....

At this point the instructor reminded the students to look at the syllabus: "Remember on the syllabus...." Then the statement, "Before, even before you even think about how you're gonna say it, you need to start thinking about what is it that I'm going to say" is indicative of Pat connecting current talk back to the "aims" she stated in her syllabus. The following passage, transcribed from her talk, further demonstrates this process:

> When you were in an academic setting, in a[n] academic setting, there are two things that are, are of great importance. First is the thesis and the second is the topic sentence. Thesis is a real big fancy word. All thesis means is main idea. Somewhere you've got to, in the beginning tell, you are reader this is my main idea. In academic writing, we start out by doing that in the beginning, usually carries the message. So in the beginning you'll get the thesis. The thesis says, this is pretty much what this stuff is about. The topic sentence usually starts out your paragraphs, and you could get a feel about where things are going by reading that first paragraph. And in, you cannot go wrong in academic writing if your first sentence or your second sentence has your topic sentence. Say to your reader this is what the paragraph is going be about. And in academic writing you ought to be able to go down and just read that first sentence and know exactly what that paper, not exactly, have a fairly good idea what that paper is about. One more time. In academic writing, your thesis, the main idea of the whole paper, book, whatever. I mean I don't know what you're writing, papers, the main idea should be in the beginning. That's the thesis, that's your main argument. Say to your reader this is what this is going to be about. And the topic sentence is the first sentence of every paragraph, and gives the reader a clear idea.

This reference to academic audience connects to the tools the instructor listed to obtain her goals. That is, the reading, writing, and evaluation of the papers; and ultimately, the students progress. We can see a reference to her syllabus again in week seven when the instructor is giving a lecture to the class:

> I would like us to share together this morning /is/ we're going to do strategy one. And when we're done, and I'll read those, share those questions with you. When we're done doing that, then you'll hand in your papers, and I'd like to begin talking about your reading on conformity. Your readings that we did. And we start working on our next paper. While at it, just to explain to you a change in the syllabus. Pull out your syllabus, syllabus if it's immediately available. We're on schedule, as far as writings are concerned. This is week seven I'm assuming.

And week twelve when talking to a student in class:

> Pat: Isn't that something? Good. All right. Two assignments for next time around. Read "Graduation" by Maya Angelou, and second—I got to find my paper. Shoot. Yeah. "Graduation" and "Custer Died for Your Sins." Pardon me. We're back to our syllabus again.
>
> Student: /?/.
>
> Pat: Yeah {laughs}. A little /jog/ out there. Now, we're back to regular old time.

Class Session as Model

This pattern of discourse can also be seen in other aspects of Pat's teaching. For example, during the second day of my observation (which was already the beginning of the third week) besides asking if everybody had a copy of her syllabus, the instructor took a few minutes to outline on the board what she wanted to accomplish for the class session, then she restated the same verbally:

> We have a double hour today, and what I'd like to do is, in the beginning, is talk about how we write sentences. Then in the second part of the session we'll talk about audience, and then address the writings that you're working on right now.

This verbal outline basically becomes her introduction to her lecture. In her opening statement—introduction—the instructor informs her students how and what she is going to cover in this first hour of the particular session; here it is the parts of a sentence, which she does. The instructor then devoted her second hour to discussing the subject of audience as she stated she was going to do. Then toward the end of the class session, there was a shift from talking about what she expected her students to do to a discussion about the writing assignment as a whole followed by a question and answer period. By allowing her students to ask questions about the assignment, Pat could restate what she has covered throughout the class session. This was a shift back to the general:

> Pat: Make sure you have in your paper your thesis. What's, what's the bottom line? What am I talking about? What is my major point in this thing? Then make sure that each paragraph begins with a sentence that summarizes what that paragraph is about. Here is big summary, thesis, and here's the paragraphs. Du, there's another one, Du, there's another one. Right here should be your topic sentence. And this says, that all the things in here, are about that. And here's the topic sentence of this one. This says, Dear Pat, this is what I'm gonna write about now, du, du, du, du, du, du. Dear Pat, this is what I'm gonna write about now. Dear Pat, this is what I'm gonna write about now. You can say it like that because that's boring, but this is going to tell my brain when I, when I go through as a reader, is going to tell my brain this is the kind of stuff that's here. These are all fruits, these are all vegetables, these are all deserts, these are all main courses. I'm, I've gotta have some kind of clue. Any questions? Yes?
>
> Student 1: Do you want us to write out our thesis when were at a /?/.
>
> Pat: No, I want to be able to know, I want to be able to find your thesis when I read your, your papers. I don't know in your first paragraph what your thesis is.
>
> Student 2: should be in here, in—
>
> Pat: Should be in, in your introduction. In your first paragraph, you should have a thesis, yes.

Pat, by restating what she had covered in her lectures, is similar to what a conclusion does in an essay, referring back to the general.

The Semester as Model

Besides looking at the syllabus and individual class lectures to demonstrate this three part discourse, this sequential and hierarchical patterning is also evident in how the instructor structures the semester. The instructor began the semester working on sentence and paragraph skills and pre writing techniques. Besides requiring students to buy an English handbook, Pat also passed out handouts on prepositions, appositives, and transitional words (see Appendix B, Punctuation and Appositives). Pat is aware that the students eventually must pay "higher attention to syntax and especially to sequential relations among sentences" (Scollon and Scollon, 1981, p. 48), and "certain words and phrases signal connections between ideas that might otherwise be missed," connections that are important to the overall understanding of the essay (Hacker, 1991, p. 104). Thus, she further supplemented the worksheets with exercises from the handbook as well.

As the semester continued, although still dealing with mechanics and punctuation, the instructor concentrated more on writing complete essays. She moved from working on sentence–level structure to the paragraphs structure and then to structuring the entire paper, hierarchically, from lower level to higher level. The first writing assignment is the descriptive/narrative essay. The topic asked the students to concentrate on themselves by describing who they were presently and where they came from in terms of culture. For the second writing assignment, though dealing with description and narrative structure, there was a shift toward exploration. This assignment centered on where the students came from in terms of migration. For the final writing assignment, analyzing an advertisement, the instructor concentrated on a more complex type of writing, the persuasive/analytical paper, what Peter Elbow (1991) calls "academic discourse" (p. 135).

The instructor, throughout the semester, consciously stressed this idea of structuring the essay according to the three part discourse pattern. In the following transcription, taken from a class session early in the semester, although the instructor does not use the word structure, she does make a number of references to structure:

> So often in writing is that we write down what's in our brains especially, if you know we talked about this whole writing, especially things that are just out front. And we have a tendency to ramble. And what you need to do now is look at your first draft, and take, in the margins put little tiny words to tell yourselves this is the main stuff that's going on here. What are the points I'm covering here? Take a look at your organization. Do you have your material? Here you have a whole list of stuff, do you have—remember how we clustered in the beginning? We—this will kind of go together. Take a look at you packages. Take a look, what do you have in this package in this first paragraph, does that all go together? What do I have in the package in the second paragraph? Does that all go together? What do I have in the package in the third paragraph? Does that all kind of go together? Once you've done reading step back and say what is this all about? What's the bottom line here? The bottom line would be your thesis. What am I trying to say here? What's

> my main point here? That's your thesis. Make sure you know what your thesis is....

Pat even gives an example of the ordering/organization she wants the students to use as she is explaining this structure to the students: "Take a look, what do you have in this package in this first paragraph...in the second paragraph...in the third paragraph?" Pat uses numbers to indicate the sequential connection between the paragraphs. Everything in the paper, however, must still connect clearly and directly to the thesis statement. The instructor is very much aware that this organizational structure is important to reading and understanding the text, as well as being able to follow the main idea of the text as shown below in a transcription of a lecture taken early in the term:

> The first day that we met we talked about the focus of this class. We'd be writing in, in the university, writing in a, in an academic setting, and colloquial, easy–going format that you have in writing a letter to a relative on whether to move to your town isn't. It's, it's a different kind of setting here than it is in that one to one, friendship that you might have with a friend or relative. When you write in an academic setting, in a academic setting, there are two things that are, are of great importance. First is the thesis and the second is the topic sentence. Thesis is a real big fancy word. All thesis means is main idea. Somewhere you've got to, in the beginning, tell your reader this is my main idea. In an academic writing, we start out by doing that in the beginning—Usually carries, carries the message. So in the beginning you'll get the thesis. The thesis says bla; this is pretty much what this stuff is about. The topic sentence usually starts out your paragraphs, and you could get a feel about where things are going by reading that first paragraph. And in, you cannot go wrong in academic writing if your first sentence or your second sentence has your topic sentence. It says to your reader this is what the paragraph is going be about. And in academic writing you ought to be able to go down and just read that first sentence and know exactly what that paper—not exactly—have a fairly good idea what that paper is about. One more time. In academic writing, your thesis, the main idea of the whole paper, book, whatever it is, I mean I don't know what you're writing, papers, the main idea should be in the beginning. That's the thesis, that's your main argument. It says to your reader this is what this is going be about, and the topic sentence is the first sentence of every paragraph, and it gives the reader a clue.
>
> When you put something down, you, you know, you put it down for a reason, unless you're just in a static trance talking and talking in /?/ whatever. Why, why did you write what you wrote when you wrote it? First of all we need a thesis. One sentence summarizing our essay's main idea. The thesis

announces our point of view on a particular subject. This is a—guys, don't get mad at the word thesis—It's not, it's not, it's not scary. Stick with me. The thesis lets the reader know what is the most important general idea. The thesis statement directs the readers' attention to the one idea which brings all the other ideas and details into perspective. It's easy stuff. You guys probably write a thesis but you don't know it. You're just so used to hearing this scary, ugly word.

Now listen to this. Writing is like taking a friend on a journey. We, first of all, tell our friends where we are going so he or she has an idea of the road ahead. That's the thesis. Then along the way we need to explain where we are going now. What this turn along the road means. That's the topic sentence.... Go to somebody's house and then say "Well, we're going to, on a journey," and then, your friend will say, "Where are we going?" You got to have, give them some kind of clue, so he knows what to take, how long you're going be gone, where you're heading for. That's your thesis. And then when you get to turn along the road you say, "Well, let's stop here I'm hungry, lets go down this path, this looks really exiting, well here's a railroad station." We gotta hop this train to get to, and so on. You got to give a person a clue to where you're going or he is just going to be blindfolded, and he's not even going to know anything about where he's been. In academic writing, most of our paragraphs must begin with a topic sentence. Topic sentences tell the reader that we are about to go on something new.

So underline the topic sentence in each paragraph. Is there, if not a topic sentence, write down at the margin what that paragraph does. Why did you write it? What kind of stuff is in, in there? Why did you write it? What does it prove? What's the point you are trying to make? Chances are you will need to put that margin stuff in the paragraph as the topic sentences. We usually have a reason for saying what we do. The task in writing is to make sure we have indicated that reason to the reader. Our audience is absent, so we can't check their body language to see if they are with us. They can't read our body language. So we need to make sure that we have filled all the gaps with our written reports. After underlining the topic sentences, go back and see if all the information in each paragraph supports that topic sentence. Did anything slide in that doesn't belong there? Do we need to leave that information or change the topic sentence? Or perhaps what, what slid in was a piece of information that needs to be developed into a separate paragraph. Then finally read the topic sentences in succession. That should provide the basic structure of what you are trying to tell your reader.

In this long transcription, Pat made a conscious effort in her teaching to provide examples of the three part organization discourse patterns, sequential and hierarchal connections, classifying, and explicitness, all of which are important characteristics to essayist literacy. She constantly stressed the major point of the session (a thesis) with sub points (the topic sentences). All are important for clarity, organization, and explicitness. When Pat used the journey metaphor, she was basically restating what is written in the handbook she recommended: "As readers move into a new paragraph, they need to know where they are—in relation to the whole essay—and what to expect in the sentences to come" (Hacker, 1991, p. 86).

In this next passage, a transcription of a class session, the students were getting ready to turn in their first papers, but before they did so, the instructor reminded the students about the structure she had emphasized earlier:

> I will then collect your first drafts. But before you do, and on your first drafts I asked you to underline your thesis, and I asked to underline your topic sentences, and I'm going to go through that and I've already given you the handout on what a thesis does and what a topic sentence does. These are umbrellas and all the stuff underneath that need to be put underneath the umbrella. So I'm going to be looking at your overall structure, and I will return those to you on Wednesday.

At this juncture, the students must demonstrate that they know what a thesis is and what topic sentences are by underlining both thesis and topic sentences in their papers. Pat was stressing to her students "what the thesis statement is to an entire paper, the topic sentence is to a paragraph" (Watkins and Dillingham, 1989, p. 272). Topic sentences supply direction and help maintain paragraph unity by keeping the organizational structure, the sequential and hierarchical structure that Pat discussed earlier. This is what the instructor is going to be looking at when she stated "So I'm going to be looking at your overall structure," when she evaluates the students' essays.

Reading Assignments as Model

Another example of how Pat stressed structure was through her reading assignments. Below is an example of a reading assignment, "What I Have Lived For" by Bertrand Russell (1967):

> Three passions, simple but overwhelmingly strong, have governed my life: the longing for love, the search for knowledge, and unbearable pity for the suffering of mankind. These passions, like great winds, have blown me hither and thither, in a wayward course, over a deep ocean of anguish, reaching to the very verge of despair.

> I have sought love, first, because love brings ecstasy–ecstasy so great that I would often have sacrificed all the rest of life for a few hours of this joy. I have sought it, next, because it relieves loneliness—that terrible loneliness in which one shivering consciousness looks over the rim of the world into the cold unfathomable lifeless abyss. I have sought it, finally, because in the union of love I have seen, in a mystic miniature, the prefiguring vision of the heaven that saints and poets have imagined. This is what I sought, and though it might seem too good for human life, this is what—at least—I have found.
>
> With equal passion I have sought knowledge. I have wished to understand the hearts of men. I have wished to know why the stars shine. And I have tried to apprehend the Pythagorean power by which number holds sway above the flux. A little of this, but not much, I have achieved.
>
> Love and knowledge, so far as they were possible, led upward toward the heavens. But always pity brought me back to earth. Echoes of cries of pain reverberate in my heart. Children in famine, victims tortured by oppressors, helpless old people a hated burden to their sons, and the whole world of loneliness, poverty, and pain make a mockery of what human life should be. I long to alleviate the evil, but I cannot, and I too suffer.
>
> This has been my life. I have found it worth living, and would gladly live again if the chance were offered me. (pp.3, 4)

Pat handed out this essay early in the semester and referred to it throughout. The primary reason she used this essay is that it follows this three part structure very clearly. There is an introduction with a clearly stated thesis: "Three passions, simple but overwhelmingly strong, have governed my life: the longing for love, the search for knowledge, and unbearable pity for the suffering of mankind." The three following paragraphs then cover each of the passions: Love, knowledge, and unbearable pity. Finally, in the concluding paragraph, "This has been my life" sums up the three main points of his life. All are written clearly and explicitly.

To Pat, when she says "structure is almost everything," she is speaking about a very specific structure, a structure that is very direct in its movement: an introduction with a clear thesis statement; a body of text that begins each paragraph with a topic sentence and ends with a transitional sentence, and finally a conclusion that restates the thesis statement and summarizes each of the main points of the paper. There is a recursive moment, a constant going back and forward. As she states:

> When we look at a picture, we see everything at once. Writing we don't. We have to start at the beginning; we have to go through—we just can't look at the individual words and figure out what it all means....Writing is linear.

> Writing starts here, writing has got to be linear... .You got to read it line by line, and word by word....

What Pat was referring to in this passage, and in her use of the word "structure," is really the organization of the essay in a specific order that is sequential and hierarchical, in this case a chronological and linear order, of the paragraphs, and sentences around a central theme, what she terms "the bottom line." The "bottom line" that the instructor was speaking about is the Western essayist literacy, the three part structure.

Metaphors as Model

In everything I have described up to now, Pat is conscious of the fact that she was stressing a particular discourse model—essayist literacy—and has developed strategies to encourage this model in her teaching. What Pat was not aware of was that she was also modeling this discourse pattern unconsciously. We can see this unconscious discourse patterning in the many metaphors Pat used in class orally. Nancy Bonvillain (1993) supports this idea. She states that "cultural meanings are additionally expressed through complex processes of semantic extensions and transfer, one such process is that of the metaphor" (p. 72). Bonvillain argues that the analyses of metaphors "provide insights into cultural constructions of reality [that] every language has characteristic conceptual metaphors which structure, not only language itself, but also particular views of reality that become shared and unconsciously assumed by its speakers" (pp. 72, 74). Thus, besides the "bottom line" analogy and the journey metaphor, there are three other metaphors that Pat referred to often: the umbrella metaphor, the train metaphor, and the sheep dog metaphor.

The Umbrella Metaphor

One of the instructor's favorite metaphors, to which she referred to quite often throughout the semester, is the umbrella metaphor:

> Uh, no, just bring your final one. Now when you bring that final one in, I want you to be able to know where the thesis is, have that underlined, and I want you to underline your topic sentences. And then you'll read, you'll be going with a partner, and your partner will say this is my topic sentence, and all this other stuff fits underneath that umbrella. Your partner will say, wow, a great job, unbelievable. We'll be looking. Yes?

This metaphor can easily be separated into three parts. The top part of the umbrella, or the "collapsible shade," represents the thesis from which the rest of the text will stem. The hinged ribs that support the collapsible shade represents the topic sentences for each paragraph; the topic sentences help maintain paragraph unity, all connected by the transitions, to the thesis, what the instructor refers to as the "center pole."

The Train Metaphor

Another one of the instructor's favorite metaphors was the train metaphor as shown in the following transcription:

> Exactly. Look at this. Look at this. This is important [Pat draws a train on chalkboard]. This is a train. I forget how to do that. [laughter]. That's the engine {Someone coughs}. {Pat draws the caboose of the train}. Here is the caboose. Here's a little guy, has his hat on. He smiling, okay. {Laughter} Now, the engine is not too good. Well, we'll have a little guide up here and he's just rolling along. Okay, there I'm happy {laughter} . There's, there's our little train. Now, here is the introduction paragraph; says choo, choo, choo, choo, choo, choo. This is what I'm going to do. Now, if you don't, and this is the paragraph, and here's a paragraph, and here's a paragraph, and here's a conclusion—bye. Now, when you're there, you're always using this choo–choo train. And if you don't connect these things, that train isn't going to go anywhere down the tracks. You're going to have an engine just wandering off all by itself. There is not going to be anything behind. Now later on I'll give you a list of transitions and the kinds of words that we use as transitions. But you have got, you have to have, well, I may not go like that, like this. You got to have a hook up. You have got to refer to this one and this one in some way, or your train isn't going to go down to the track....

Although I see this metaphor as a conscious effort to maintain a single idea in a single direction throughout the text, interestingly, when the instructor drew the train on the chalkboard, she drew the engine, three cars, and the caboose unconsciously. The engine represents the introduction; each car following represents the different paragraphs and the caboose represents the concluding paragraph. All are connected by the transitions, what Pat described as the "hook ups."

The Sheep Dog Metaphor

We can see this idea of a single topic moving in a single direction in Pat's sheep dog metaphor:

> Writing is like a Scottish sheep dog bringing in the sheep: she races back and forth, driving the flock in one direction signaled by the shepherd but acting in response to the developing occasions, nudging here, circling there, rushing back to round up a stray, dashing ahead to cut off an advance in the wrong direction.

When writing, the writer becomes the shepherd. The sheep dog is the main topic whose job is to keep the paper focused on one subject, and the sheep are the details being organized into this beginning, middle, and end discourse model.

Conclusion

As the semester came to an end, although I was not surprised that the instructor summarized to the class what was to transpire over the final days of the semester, I was surprised about what she said:

> In the first hour of Wednesday, I will be reviewing, going over Bedford things with you. Some things in your Bedford grammar book that we have not talked about yet that I want to make sure you know before you leave. I'm not going to assign any Bedford because I think that you possibly have to finish up your papers. That's Wednesday. The second hour Wednesday, I will give you the evaluations, which all students and all classes must do for their instructors. So that will be the second hour. And then I thought that maybe we could meet cause I'll be leaving /?/. If that's okay with you. This coming Wednesday, paper due. This—we're talking about in two days. Your paper is due in two days. And in two days, I will give you what your final essay is going to be on. That essay will happen on December 2nd. It's a Monday. You'll come into class. You will have one hour. You will write your final exam. Okay. And then you'll sign up, if you want a chance to talk to me, on Wednesday. On Wednesday there will not be class. There will just be conferences. So I will set aside the two hours that we normally have on Wednesday the 4th as conference time. Whether you come for conferences will not affect your grade whatsoever, so don't think you have to come here to get brownie points. That's, it's—no, I will, will tell. I think sometimes you wonder, and I think it's important to know. So I don't mean that in any kind of vicious kind of way. But I will set aside time, and, and on Monday the 2nd, I'll give you time to sign up, so you don't have to be around here and wait. So on Monday, the 2nd, you'll sign up for a conference time if you want on the 4th. I will be here. That conference time will be, go over your final paper. If you have any questions about, we may, for us to talk about your writing

> together. And I can tell you what your grade is going to be. And most of you ought to have a fairly good idea of what your grade is even at this point. Yes?

By stating "I will be reviewing, going over Bedford things with you. Some things in your Bedford grammar book that we have not talked about yet that I want to make sure you know before you leave," the instructor has successfully reduced teaching back to what Henry Giroux (1992) refers to "a narrowly defined concern with instrumental techniques, skills, and objectives," meaning, ultimately, that the focus is still going to be on punctuation and grammar (p. 98). This is further compounded because it was she, the instructor, who was going to evaluate the papers. As she stated in her "Grading" section of the syllabus: "The final grade for the course will be based on the six graded writings (90%) and in class writing (10%)." This is further compounded by the fact that if they "miss more than four" class meeting, they will fail the course.

In the end, the students are not being evaluated on how well they do and what they have learned, but on what they do wrong. Better yet, on how well they can avoid mistakes. This further suggests a rationale for the pervasiveness (and function) of this structure in education, especially when teaching to minority students, in particular Latino students (Ybarra, 2001).

Notes

1. Luckily, the instructor had not handed out or gone over her class syllabus until the second week of the semester. For the first week of class, Pat concentrated on the diagnostic essay for the first and second class meeting, and the computer session was on the third meeting.
2. I edited this transcription, as I will do for many of the transcriptions I use, for false starts, pauses, etc., to make the transcriptions clearer.
3. A "register" is defined "as a conventionalized way of speaking used in particular situations" (Heath, 1978, p. 2) "whose stylistic characteristics are recognizable when used outside its defining context, but which is used primarily within that defining context" (Farr, 1992, p. 6).

CHAPTER 3

Cultural Dissonance

> Before dismissing urban, U.S.–born youth as lazy underachievers, it behooves researchers and practioners to first examine the school's role in fostering poor academic performance. Bringing schools into sharper focus, as my study does, reveals that U.S–born youth are neither inherently antischool nor oppositional. They oppose a schooling process that disrespects them; they oppose not education, but schooling.
>
> —Valenzuela, 1999, p.5

Introduction

In Chapter 2, I revealed the structural barriers within academia that limit student participation in ways that are culturally and linguistically unfamiliar and alienating to Latino students. In this chapter, I will trace and map the anger, alienation, and frustration of the four Latino students in the class and show how these emotions and attitudes are created and brought into existence by and through the educational system itself. I show how learning to write academic papers is not a smooth transition over the course of the semester, but rather a hostile and invasive course of action which ultimately leaves a negative impression on Latino students about writing and contribute highly to what I term "'cultural dissonance' to highlight issues of cultural differences and dominance in the context of English/writing courses in higher education. In doing so, I expose the larger hidden curriculum of assimilation (Ybarra, 2001, p. 46). I offer this concept of cultural dissonance, a term that I took from the more frequently used notion of cognitive dissonance, to highlight issues of cultural differences in ways of thinking between many minority groups and the academia (Ybarra, 2001, p.46).

Awkward Situations

I begin with Connie, an entering freshman and eighteen years of age, who categorized herself ethnically as half Ecuadorian and half Argentine.[1] Her mother is from Ecuador and her father from Argentina, but neither parent had been back to their respective countries for twenty five years. She was born and reared in the United States and attended both public and private schools here for twelve years—Connie has never left the Cicero area.[2] She took advance English courses in high school, yet she scored low on her written portion of her placement test and was placed in Basic Writing. She did not speak Spanish except for a word here and there.

Letty was also an entering freshman. She categorized herself as Mexican. She, too, was eighteen. Letty's parents were born and raised in Mexico and emigrated to the United States a year before Letty was born. Letty attended school in both California and Chicago since she was five years of age. She and her parents go to Mexico on a regular basis—at least once a year. In fact, her family was already planning to go to Mexico during Christmas break at the end of the semester. Letty was in Basic Writing because she did not score high enough on the written portion of her placement exam to enter the required composition class.

Juan was a senior, older than the other three Latino students, at twenty six years of age. He identified himself as Latin. He was born and raised in Mexico and had only been in the United States—Chicago—for about four years. He not only had been attending UIC for four years, but also had a couple of years of college in Mexico. He registered for Basic Writing because he wanted to sharpen his writing skills. He, in fact, did not take the placement test, nor did he have to because he was never officially registered in the course. What he did was make an agreement with the instructor to sit in her class and do the entire course work, which he did.

Finally, after I had a chance to go over the release forms privately, I added one more student to my list of subjects, Joe.[3] The only information I have on Joe was what he gave me on the release form. He was an entering freshman—eighteen and just out of high school. He categorized himself as Hispanic. The reason I had trouble identifying him as Latino was because of his physical characteristics: blond hair, blue eyes, white complexion, and no discernable accent that could be attributed to being a Latino. The reason I have very little information on him, besides what he listed on the release form, is because from when I started observing the class, he only attended two other class sessions besides this first one: once during week three and once during week seven, when he was asked to drop the course.

Because of these differences, each Latino/a student presented different, sometimes awkward and sometimes problematic, types of situations for the instructor. And because of my experience in teaching Basic Writing and my ethnicity, I was also put in very awkward positions several times during my research, something I was trying to avoid. This conflicted with the role I was trying to assume, that of a tutor and observer. At times I felt that my ethnicity would influence the behavior of the student, so I would not be able to "maintain some of the detached objectivity" which is so important to research (Saville Troike, 1989, p. 109). Though difficult, objectivity is essential in ethnographic research. Still, these characteristics allowed me insights about the Latino students and about what they brought into class, which allowed me to analyze each of the following awkward situations.

Connie

The first awkward event happened during week four of the semester. During weeks one and two, Pat centered her lectures around the parts of essays, structuring sentences and paragraphs. At the beginning of week three, Pat assigned her first essay. The topic centered around defining cultural expectations, specifically: How cultural expectations happen and why? When do they happen? What are the effects cultural expectations have on a person?

On this particular day, Pat started the class by handing back a draft of the first essay and then gave a brief lecture about what to concentrate on—essay structure:

> I did not take the time and the space to write the encouraging comments that your papers deserve. What I did is point out general weaknesses, so when you look at, doesn't look and say, "Oh she didn't like and she didn't like that." I well liked a lot of what you did. What I was trying to do on this first draft is point out things that you need to work on. So do not take this in depressed, /or/, negative connotation. These are things for you to /?/ as we're just working. This is your first draft that you need to work on right now. So don't be sad, don't be depressed, don't feel that what you did, what you did was not good. I was pleased with, I was delighted with the amount of information you had. I thought that there was a lot of thinking, a lot of good questioning, and I'm guessing that the kind of questions that we asked together in the class and the kinds of talking that we did really helped you pull things out of your mind because there was a wealth of material in your papers. I was just delighted

> with that. The biggest thing, and I'm changing our course of work right now, the biggest thing that we need to work on /in/ this class and the next class is structure. And what I'm going to ask you to do today is—I'm going to return these papers to you, you can take a minute, at the most, to read my comments. And my comments are scattered because I want to take individual time to talk to you personally. By the time I sit down and write things out, I have more writing than you have paper, and that's silly. I'd much rather take time with you individually to talk about it, and then you can answer me back, and we can go somewhere with it, rather than a one way dialogue with my writing comments on your paper. So those kinds of things are sketches, and I put words in the margins so that I would know what I wanted to talk to you about it. So don't feel that you need to make sense out of my sketchy remarks because they're sketchy. When the two of us sit down together, we can talk about your paper. But generally, throughout the class, we need to work on structure.

Pat then asked the students to pair up and read and discuss each other's papers:

> Now what I'd like you to do, read the comments that I wrote, then find a partner. Sit next to the partner, and I want partners of two. Listen carefully. Read your paper out loud to your partner…and share with your partner. See if that is what your partner heard. Then switch the process….Once you've gone through this process, start working with it, start molding it. It's like taking little pieces of clay and putting it, see, see what kind of central form you can come up with. And I would like to spend some time today talking with you individually on, on your writing. And then working on it. Today is Wednesday, and then working on it together in class on Friday, so you can keep on forming this stuff. You have all the ingredients out….

Pat then began walking from group to group, beginning at one end of the room, spending roughly five minutes with each pair of students and then gradually moving on to the next pair of students. She slowly made her way around the room. I, like the instructor, also walked around the room, but I did not join in any of the discussions. I just listened to the different groups as I came to each group. I started on the opposite side of the room that Pat had started on and met up with her around the center. There she stopped and leaned toward me and asked (whispered to) me to work with Connie and Letty. At this time, I didn't think anything unusual about what I was asked to do. I just thought it was part of my role as tutor, and I was delighted to have been given an assigned role. I moved the tape recorder over to where Connie and Letty were sitting and asked, "Do you want me to work with both of you?" Both nodded, and so I slid my chair over.

For the first few minutes, I interacted with Letty, but Letty was set in what she needed to do (work on structuring her essay). I switched over to Connie. I found that Connie had not even turned in a draft. In fact, she hadn't written anything. I thought it was because she did not understand the topic and this is why she was concentrating on her math. So for the next fifteen minutes I explained the topic to her. The following passage is part of that discussion:

> Connie: I'm /confused/. Am I going to talk about just rules on how to behave?
> Raul: Well, no. You got to narrow it down.
> Letty: You could put just like, uh, who influenced you in these roles on how to behave. Now these rules were influenced by parents—
> Connie: Parents?
> Letty: Friends.
> Raul. So we have different sets of rules, right?
> Connie: Hmm.
> Raul: Your parents' rules. Who else are forcing rules on you?
> Connie: School.
> Raul: School. Who else?
> Connie: My job.
> Raul: Job. Who else?
> Connie: Friends.
> Raul: Friends. Who else?
> Connie: And myself.
> Raul: And yourself.
> Connie: Look, I want to put in like, my mother like objected to the American culture too. Like, before she never used to let us do anything, but now she does.
> Raul: Okay, so she changes the rules.
> Connie: Yeah.
> Raul: Which in turn, what happens? /?/ change rules yourself.
> Connie: Yeah, I suppose. Those are the rules I wanted so.
> Raul: Okay, yeah.
> Connie: To change myself.
> Raul: Yeah, we're very /selective/ in what rules we accept in ourselves.
> Connie: But how do I fit all that into like, a thesis, or whatever?
> Raul: Yeah. But now we're talking about, culture…is being used /?/.
> Connie: Can I put "in society" or will that be wrong? Or just "to behave?"
> Raul: No, that's right—To behave in society. Then you have to say—explain what you mean by rules. And eventually you got to narrow it down to something very specific.

Connie: How do I narrow rules down?

Raul: Well, you define them. What do you mean by rules on how to behave? What do you mean by that? Actually, I should say what do you mean by rules?

Connie: What do I mean by rules? Like, there are certain ways to, to behave like—

Raul: Okay, maybe that—

Connie: With friends—

Raul: Yeah. Let me give you an example. Has somebody ever sat down with you and said, these are the rules that we are going to live by.

Connie: No.

Raul: Why—so how did you pick them up?

Connie: By, they told me, like it is.

Letty: The way you see /things/ maybe now?

Connie: I don't know.

Raul: Did they /?/?

Letty: Well, you know, you follow their example.

Raul: Okay, by, by example we pick up a lot of things. Do your parents work hard? Are they a hard working family?

Connie: Yeah.

Raul: Isn't that what kind of rubbed off on you?

Connie: Yeah.

Raul: Yeah. So you know you need to work hard. That's a rule that you picked up. Nobody told you that.

Connie: But how do I write that down though? I don't know.

Raul: Well, just like this. Just expand. You're not explaining specifics. I'm giving you specifics, but you're not explaining your specifics. You're explaining general right now. Rules. So what are these rules?

Connie: I don't know.

Raul: If you don't know what rules are, where can we go to find out?

Connie: Where can we go to find out?

Letty: Maybe you should ask—

Connie: We /check/ like in school, and–

Raul: And what book did, can we go to find out? Another word for rules?

Connie: The dictionary I guess.

Raul: And what else?

Connie: The thesaurus.

Raul: Thesaurus.

Connie: Yeah. /?/. And what am I supposed to do with that.

Raul: Well, you're trying to figure out—

Connie: Define rules with that?

Raul: Define rules.

Connie: Just from the dictionary like that? Aren't we supposed to write what we think it is?

Raul: Well, the only thing we get to /?/ that we have to /?/. A lot of what you know, not, not only came from talking to your parents, talking to your friends, going to school. It also came from reading. It came from watching TV.

Connie: Oh yeah.

Raul: It came from. It came from all kinds of things. So, do we look at the /?/, we don't combine, how to define. We have to use all those sources to help.

Connie: And so, the—

Raul: Well, what are rules?

Connie: I don't know how to say it. I can't—

Raul: Okay, so where do we go to find out how to say it?

Connie: I guess the dictionary.

Raul: The dictionary and?

Connie: Thesaurus. See, it's not telling you anything you already don't know. I don't —

Raul: But it's giving you different ways to say it.

Connie: So I'm going to say like culture to me is rules, and how to be in society. And I'll say "rules are." Like telling them like. I don't know.

Raul: Yeah, no. That's a great main point. That's the whole idea. That's the whole idea. Write down everything you—{there is a lot shuffling of chairs}.

At this point, I realized that the class was over and was letting out. I also knew that I had not helped Connie solve her problem about what to write. Every time she said, "I don't know," I heard and felt Connie's frustration. I wanted to continue working with her, so I was very happy (and surprised) that before she left she indicated that she, along with Letty, wanted to continue talking to me about her essay:

Connie: Yeah. Hopefully, {Giggles}, I'm, I'm going to try to write my rough draft today. Are you going to be in the Writing Center tomorrow?

Raul: Yeah, I'll be there in the morning. I'm also in there in the morning on Fridays. I'm there about every day.

Letty: Just in the morning or?

Raul: Yeah, no, no, not just in the morning. If you go in there, let's say you walk through the door, and you look on the wall. There's a schedule of when I'm there.

Letty: Okay.

Raul: Ask somebody there. And, I'm there quite a bit. And I'll be more than happy to sit there and talk to you and help you out with your paper.

Letty: Okay.
Raul: Yours too (To Connie).
Connie: Okay, thanks.

After class, after everyone had gone, Pat asked me to turn off the tape recorder, so I did. This was the first time Pat had asked me to turn off the tape recorder. Later, I noticed that every time she wanted to talk to me about a student she would asked me to turn off the tape recorder. She never gave a reason why and I never quite felt comfortable asking her about it. She then asked me general questions about my work with Connie, about how Connie responded to my working with her. I told her that Connie seemed to have problems with the topic, but I thought that she was beginning to understand. I also told Pat that I was going to meet with Connie before the next class session, to continue helping her with her paper. Pat then confided to me that she had trouble talking to Connie, for that matter, even approaching her. She followed by telling me that she was concerned about Connie's attitude about class and about her passing the class because Connie had not turned in a draft of her essay.

I was bothered by this. I didn't notice any hostility from Connie, just frustration indicated by Connie saying "I don't know." When I returned to my office I went over the tape from this class session several times and counted the number of times Connie said "I don't know." It was twenty–one times in the course of fifteen minutes. During this counting process, I came across a passage that indicated a possible answer to her frustration:

Connie: But this just a paper on cultural ex, expectations.
Raul: What are your expectations?
Connie: I don't know.
Raul: But this is what you understood then? That this is a paper on cultural expectations?
Connie: Yeah, but, my culture doesn't. I don't know. I don't know. My culture has, not, my background, has nothing to do with me 'cause I really don't care. Well, like {Giggles}. I don't know.
Raul: You don't care about what?
Connie: About Ecuadorian cultural, Argentine, because I really don't—my dad doesn't know. I don't know.

Then I recalled something she had said earlier, and I rewound the tape to that point on the audiotape:

> Connie: …just culture expectations. I didn't know I had culture. I don't know. And, and you got to like, they might seem like, they have like—I don't know. I really don't have—but that's what culture thinks,

Then a few minutes later, she says something similar:

> Connie: I don't think I have a culture, in that—

After listening to these passages several times, I realized that Connie was not having problems with the specific topic or with writing, but rather something much broader. Connie was having trouble with her own cultural identity. As the passage above and below indicate, she did not see herself as having, or belonging to an Ecuadorian or Argentinean background—that is her parents background:

> Connie: Yeah, but, my culture doesn't. I don't know. I don't know. My culture has, not, my background, has nothing to do with me 'cause I really don't care. Well, like {Giggles}. I don't know.
>
> Raul: You don't care about what?
>
> Connie: About Ecuadorian cultural, Argentine, because I really don't—my dad doesn't know. I don't know.

How Connie is attempting to define herself is not by who she is, but by who she is not; she is not Ecuadorian and she is not Argentinean. Moreover, as she said in the next passage, she is not "white" nor is she "dark" either. I understood now why she was having trouble with the topic and why she was frustrated. Connie could not write about cultural expectations because she did not know who she was. This explains the "I don't know." As David Bartholomae (1988a) argues, "When the writer says, 'I don't know,' then he is not saying that he has nothing to say, he is saying that he is not in a position to carry on this discussion" (p. 277). Connie could not and would not be able to write effectively because she could not "extend herself…into the commonplaces, set phrases, rituals and gestures, habits of mind, tricks of persuasion, obligatory conclusions, and necessary connections that determine the 'what might be said'" because she did not feel herself to be an "insider" (Bartholomae, 1988a, p. 281). She could not extend herself into those places described because she was not sure of who she was:

> All writers, in order to write, must imagine for themselves the privilege of being "insiders"—that is, the privilege both of being inside the establishment and powerful discourse and of being granted a special right to speak. (Bartholomae, 1988b, p. 278)

In my realizing this, I knew then what to concentrate on for our next conversation; not so much as to have her define herself culturally or ethnically, but to let her know that it was all right to be confused about her cultural identity. That she should concentrate on who she is now. As Raymond Padilla and Rudolfo Chávez Chávez (1993) argue, to value who she is now because "in this context, valuing the self becomes vital to personal and academic survival" (p. 10). This is what I tried to do the following day when she came to talk to me again:

Raul: Okay, that's a good point. Culture is never what they call static. It's always changing, always....But do you consider yourself American?
Connie: I, yeah, because I was born here.
Raul: Is that the only reason?
Letty: No, because, like, you hold American values also.
Raul: You hold American values?
Letty: I mean, not values, I mean, American—
Raul: When you think of American, what do you think of?
Connie: Someone who—I don't know.
Letty: There isn't really an American—
Raul: No?
Letty: Because what everybody calls—
Raul: But what is it, when somebody, I'm not thinking what everybody else thinks. I want to know what you think when somebody tells you, American.
Connie: I don't know.
Raul: What do you think of?
Connie: Born here, whites {laughs}. Whites.
Raul: Or Anglos, right?
Connie: Unless they get tanned {laughs again}.
Raul: But that's one way a lot of people look at it when they see Americans. I mean—
Connie: I know it's not right, but—
Raul: No, that doesn't matter because there is no right or wrong in this case, but that's what you think of when somebody says it: "What's an American?" Now, do you consider yourselves that?
Connie: I'm not that white, but I'm not that dark either. {Laughs}.
Raul: No, but do you consider yourself that?

Connie: No.

Raul: No. Because that's not your image of yourself, right? So what is the image of yourself?

Connie: I don't know /?/, I don't know.

Raul: If someone asks you what, what are you? What's your ethnic background?" What would you say?

Connie: My dad is from Ecuador, and my mom is from Argentina. That's what I always tell them.

Raul: All right. That tells me something, all right. You do not say where you're from, but you say where your parents are from.

Connie: Yeah.

Raul: Okay. Why?

Connie: Because, I don't know. I just always I say that.

Raul: Why? Now, I'm not disagreeing with you. I just want to find that reason, why.

Connie: I guess I don't consider myself, like, Argentinean/Ecuadorian because I wasn't born, you know, there.

Raul: Okay. That's a good reason. You weren't born there.

Connie: Just my parents /were born/ from there. I was born here.

Raul: Let me ask you this question. Why do you find yourself having trouble defining who you are?

Connie: Because I wasn't, because I can't say I'm American, because I was American, you know. And I was not born in another country, so it's hard for me to say that. I don't know.

Raul: Okay, so, you're struggling, right?

Connie: I don't know {laughs}.

Raul: Every time somebody asks you this question, you have to think about it. And the easiest way to get around that, is say what?

Connie: Where my parents are from.

Raul: Yeah. That doesn't say who you are.

Connie: No.

Raul: No?

Connie: Oh, they get the idea {laughs}.

Although I knew that Connie's identity struggle was not solved nor was it going to be solved in one semester, I did feel the tension ease quite a bit, especially when she laughed. I didn't sense her frustration like I had a few days before, and she was able to write her essay.[4] I talked to Pat after this incident about not being sure if my working with Connie individually was the best way to go about handling this problem that she was having with Connie. I thought it best if she talked to Connie about this herself. Nevertheless, Pat insisted that I continue working on a one on one basis with Connie because she didn't think she could—because the one time she did have a conference with Connie, Connie seemed "hostile" toward her.

Joe

The next awkward situation happened at the beginning of the seventh week of the semester and it involved Joe. I never got to know Joe because a major problem was that he was often absent from class. During the first five weeks of the semester, Joe attended three class sessions. The first time I saw Joe was the first day of classes when I asked the students to fill out the student questionnaire—a short survey where I asked the students to state their name, age, gender, language, and ethnicity. I had trouble identifying him as Latino because of his phenotype. Joe was an entering freshman, eighteen, just out of high school: blond hair, blue eyes, light skin complexion, and no discernable accent that could be attributed to his being a Latino.

Because the day I passed out the questionnaire was the first day of the semester, most of the time was taken up by the instructor for the introduction of the course and of herself; I never had the opportunity to talk to any of the students. Later that day while looking over the questionnaires at the point where I asked the students to identify themselves ethnically, I came upon Joe. There were a total of fourteen students in the class: four classified themselves as African American, two as Filipino, two as Italian, four as Latino/Hispanic, and two as white. Joe was one of the four who categorized himself as "Hispanic."

The second time Joe attended class was the Monday of week three—he had previously missed four consecutive class sessions. Joe only spoke up once during the entire class session that day and that was when Pat directed a comment to him about his being in class. The class was already five weeks into the semester, but this was only Joe's second time attending class. I was concerned about Joe's absences for two reasons. First, because of what Pat had written in her syllabus:

> It is important that you attend regularly and participate in class activities. Class time will involve instruction, discussion, writing workshops, and individual assistance. All of these are essential to your growth as a writer. Therefore, more than four absences will be grounds for failure.

Joe had reached the maximum number of absences allowed, four. After four, Pat would have every right to fail Joe. Second, because of his many absences, Joe never had an opportunity to become part of the classroom community. As many scholars have noted, an important part of the students' integration into college is the interaction that takes places between students and between students and faculty. Likewise, instructors play an important role in helping students become members of the school community. Other than the short monologue at the beginning of class, there was no real dialogue between Joe and Pat.

Pat began the class session by taking roll. She appeared surprised that Joe was in class. She then referred to her syllabus first to indicate that the class was on schedule according to her syllabus, and to make a minor change, eliminating, by one, the number of essays to be assigned (see Appendix A, Syllabus). Then there was a question–and–answer period in which Pat answered questions students had about past assignments. The students had just finished writing their second essay, but before collecting the essays, Pat wanted the students to practice editing each other's papers.

After about ten minutes Pat asked the students to break into pairs and question each other about the essays using a list of questions Pat had written on the chalkboard to help the students analyze each other's papers:

> These are the questions, and you'll be sharing with one partner or two with whatever you're comfortable with as far as your getting in a group. One, what do you think I am trying to say? Two, what did you like best about my writing? Three, did any part made you stop and read it again in order to understand what I meant? Four, did I choose enough examples or details for you to understand what I mean? Five, is it clear each time, where I started a new paragraph? Six, without looking at the writing again, what part of it do you remember the best? Seven, what questions do you still have about this piece of writing? Now, if there is a major change or, or little changes that you want to make, you may do that before you turn it in to me. I want to say this till your final draft because you've worked on this draft and with my help on the first draft, and you've worked on this, and now I'm assuming, hopefully, that you will feel confident with what you've done, and I'd like you to go back and forth to see how what you feel confident with is experienced by another reader. And so you begin dialoguing with that, and you're not only dialoguing with me on how you're doing on expressing your thoughts in writing. So this way you can feel good what you have in front of you because this is your final draft, and then get feedback from another reader on how well you're presenting your ideas so that they're clear to your reading partners. Any questions? Is that clear? Okay, let's get into groups. Whatever you're

> comfortable with, with two or three. Start going through these questions on one another's paper—and what do you think, twenty minutes? Should that do it? Maybe fifteen. Let's go. Do it.... How are we breaking up into partners, so I can make sense of this? So it's those two....

All the students paired up, except Joe, so I decided to pair up with him. Before we started working, however, Pat asked to talk to me outside the classroom. After we had both walked out into the hallway, Pat—after taking a couple of deep breaths—asked me to talk to Joe about his dropping the course because of his being absent for so long. Pat's concern with Joe was that he had missed too many classes.

As in the incident with Connie, I was hesitant to get directly involved in handling the situation, but Pat felt I would be better suited to handle talking to Joe because of Joe's and my similar cultural backgrounds, i.e., we were both Latino. Also because of my experience teaching Basic Writing, she felt that I was better prepared to avert a confrontation. I could agree to being better prepared, but I was not sure that I should be the one to suggest that Joe drop the course. I felt I was moving beyond my role of tutor. I was going beyond the parameters of a peer relationship, a peer helper, and into a position of authority where I was now responsible for evaluating and assessing student performance. This was something I did not want to do, but Pat insisted, and I gave in. She then went back into the class and returned a few seconds later with Joe. I knew that taking on this new role would make approaching Joe more difficult, if not impossible, to talk to him about why he was missing class so much.

As I stood there in the hallway, I could only speculate about how Joe would feel when asked to drop. Twelve years before, as an undergraduate taking Basic Writing, I too was asked to drop a Basic Writing course because I too had missed a lot of classes because I was struggling with writing. What the instructor saw were only my absences; what he didn't see was my working more than forty hours a week; what he didn't see was my struggling with my own identity; what he didn't see was my feeling like I didn't belong. And when he asked me to drop the course—and even college completely—I felt like I was not very bright and that I would never complete college because I didn't belong. I wondered if this is what would happen to Joe?

Pat returned a few minutes later with Joe.[5] As I suspected, Joe responded angrily to my suggesting to him that he drop the course. He felt that he was not given a fair chance. I explained to him again that he was being asked to drop because of the number of absences he had and nothing else. I repeated to him several times that this was only a suggestion. If he felt strongly enough, he could stay in the course. No one could force him to drop the course. He kept insisting, however, that we were unfairly singling him out. After about five to ten minutes, Joe did agree, but he stated that he was not happy with what I was telling him, and that he was going to relay all that we had discussed to his adviser. I told him that would be an excellent idea. Throughout the entire interaction, Pat kept silent.

As with the situation with Connie, not only did I feel bad about going beyond my role as tutor, about having to ask Joe to drop the course, but I was also very upset that Pat had put me in such a position. I had a very difficult time dealing with Joe dropping the course. I felt as though I had failed him. I hated that I was the one to ask Joe to drop the course, but I was more upset that the instructor had put me in such a position.

When I got home, I reviewed the audiotape from the one other time he attended class to see if there was anything I could have done. I noticed that the last time Joe had attended class was the Monday of week three. He only spoke up one time during the entire class session and that was when Pat directed a comment to him about his being in class this particular day:

> Pat: {Begins the session by taking roll. She calls out the names of the students, and the students respond by saying "here" or raising their hand. When she gets to Joe's name she stops and says}. You look like you slept well, Joe. No more partying, or are you taking care of yourself?
>
> Joe: Yeah, no more partying.
>
> Students: {laugh}.
>
> Pat: (Goes back to taking roll).

Although, this interaction was very short, it took place in a humorous tone, and the class laughed at Joe's response. I noted in my notes that Joe himself did not laugh. Pat also did not appear surprised at his response. As far as Joe was concerned, his suspicions were confirmed—he did not belong—he was not welcomed in this classroom.

A few days after this incident, I attempted to contact Joe at his home, but I received no response to the messages and letters I sent him.[7] Later, I found that Joe not only dropped the class, but also dropped out of college completely. Joe left the class (or was forced to do so) due to a cultural chasm that separated him from the teacher. Afterward, I did tell Pat that I wanted to talk to her about Joe, about what transpired, and about how I could have handled the situation differently. Although Pat never outright told me that she did not want to talk to me about what happened or about Joe, she always managed to evade discussing the incident.

Looking back at this scenario, I realized that the instructor had adapted a strategy in which she thought she was helping Joe without considering how deeply this way of thinking was entrenched in his psyche and how this manifested itself in the classroom—that is, in her teaching and in her personal evaluation of Joe. All she saw were the absences, the missed classes. She did not see Joe. She did not know who he was nor understood why he was missing class. It is obvious that we failed to help Joe and failed in helping many students like Joe because we did not take the time to find out what he was going through (Ybarra, 2001, p. 46).

Letty

I found it interesting that these two students, Connie and Joe, both Latino and both with similar attitudes about the class, though neither wanted to be in this Basic Writing course, each responded differently to the class. Connie responded by showing what Pat referred to as "hostility." Joe just didn't come to class. Connie did try to understand the topics assigned. In fact, in one of her statements to me she says, "Just tell me what you want me to do, and I'll do it."[6] For her effort, she received a B for the course. Joe, on the other hand, not only dropped the course, but also discontinued going to any of his other classes.[7] Both of these students' reactions were quite different from the reaction of the other two subjects, Letty and Juan.

As the following segment shows, Letty actively participated in class discussions and she turned in all her work on time:

Pat: What would happen, Student 1, if everybody got born, and we had people running around all over the place and there was no culture? What would happen?

Student 1: You couldn't really tell anybody apart.

Pat: You couldn't, you couldn't tell anybody apart. That, that's true.

Student 2: To me it's like some people are different than others because of her cultural background.

Pat: Okay, good. So you could tell people apart by culture. It gives you an identity. So it, it may, it may not be able to tell people apart it may give you a sense of an identity. This is who I am, this is where I fit. Every single human being that, that is born into this world eventually gets old enough to look around and say where do I fit—Every single human being, from primitive men right on up—Where do I fit? What does this all mean? What, what's, what's this all about? Culture gives an answer to that. Yes?

Letty: /?/ You're saying to yourself, even—
Pat: Real loud so we can hear you.
Letty: In the culture {clears throat} uh, even though those people that, like that, know what, like know what their real culture is, usually they're adopted. They grow up with the, the culture of that person that they grew up with
Pat: Exactly.
Letty: They need that background in order to, they need it to fulfill something in their lives.
Pat: Yeah, and, and fulfilling something in life might be where do I fit. What's expected of me? How am I supposed to act? What's important? It's the real thing. Like with my daughter in college last night. She was in tears and all upset. We talked about the basic questions in life, what's important? It's cultural values? Yes?
Student 3: Hum, it doesn't because it, well it what Letty was saying about, you grow up in that culture, and then you fall back on it, it helps you realize what your own beliefs are and, and you have a sense of what kind of morality—
Pat: Yeah.

Letty's biggest problem was writing her essays according to the structure Pat wanted the students to follow. Interestingly enough, on Letty's first essay, the only comment Pat wrote was "excellent." On Letty's second essay, Pat wrote this comment: "Work on focusing everything you say through your thesis. "Reread & #4 and ask yourself why you included that info. Next time, make info connection clear to reader." What Pat is asking Letty to do is to reread the paper and on why she included information on "values in paragraph four." On the third essay, Pat wrote this comment: "Keep working on your flow of thought." (For a complete copy of Letty's second essay, see Appendix D.) As the following passages show, most of my conversations with Letty dealt with structuring paragraphs:

Raul: That's it. And now just go on from there. What it means, rules and how to behave. And you're dealing with this—
Letty: Like a lot of things. And it, and see that what I don't. She says to put a thesis based on sense of time.
Raul: Don't worry about the thesis now. You can always stick it at the very—
Letty: This is my thesis.
Raul: /?/.
Letty: Rules.
Raul: All right.

Letty: And it's because I have, like, first of all I'm, I'm doing it in general 'cause it—

Raul: Okay.

Letty: Like I have, "All parents have cultural expectations, but not everyone has the same one that all people are the same. My cultural expectations came from family background and myself."

Raul: There's your introduction to your thesis right there. Now you're ready to begin your paper.

Letty: But how do I fit everything under there because then I start talking in general, like—

Raul: Okay, you don't—

Letty: Images of one should be?

Raul: No, See, you want to get away from general.

Letty: So, what would I do about the background? See, there's so many images of how one should be. How so we know which one is the best one?

Raul: Okay, that was a good start. Let's go back to your, to your thesis. What is it?

Letty: "All people have cultural expectations, but not everyone has the same ones because not all people are the same."

Raul: Okay.

Letty: What if I stated that—

Raul: Now read the whole thing.

Letty: Yeah, I will.

Raul: Read the whole thing.

Letty: My cultural expectations came form my family, friends, and myself.

Raul: Okay. Let's stop right there. Now, let's say this is the beginning of the paper. What are you going to write about in your paper?

Letty: I'm going to write about my cultural expectations, which came from my family, and friends, and myself.

Raul: Yeah, you now need to expand on those three things. That's what you need to write on. See that? Everything goes back to that.

Letty: I mean, I have all the ideas, but it's harder to put it down in words.

Raul: Well, except. Look at your thesis. You have a nice thesis there. And I would start with that. The first thing, of course, I would start with yourself. "I." This is what, this is who I am. Introduce yourself. And then go from there.

As the two previous passages show, Letty always appeared eager, interested, and willing to cooperate and worked hard at improving her essays. I was sure she would do okay grade wise and that she enjoyed being in the class.

I by chance ran into Letty two semesters after she had completed Basic Writing. She had also completed her freshman writing requirement, taken in the spring semester at UIC, and her research class, at a community college over the summer. Overall, Letty had done very well in her English and composition courses, so I was surprised about Letty's response to my questions concerning this Basic Writing course.

> Raul: I want to get your reactions about writing now to see how you feel about it?
> Letty: Okay.
> Raul: Have you taken English 160?
> Letty: 160.
> Raul: What grade did you get?
> Letty: B.
> Raul: How about 161?
> Letty: 161 I took that over the summer. And I took that at a community college, and I got an A. . . .

After a few minutes when I thought she had relaxed enough, I focused on the Basic Writing course she had taken with Pat:

> Raul: Why were you in 151?
> Letty: That's where I was placed
> Raul: Were you upset?
> Letty: Oh yeah, because I was thinking, why do I have to go backwards instead of forward. Because, you know, everybody places in 160, and so just because of an essay that they give you, which is basically not all that great, you know. I ended up writing like a paragraph. And then it was timed, so I didn't have time. I was just trying to think about what to write about and time was up /?/.

Letty's final grade in the Basic Writing course was a B while in English 160 she received a B and English 161 an A. When I asked her how she did in her first semester overall—including her other courses—this was her response:

> Letty: I didn't do too bad. I didn't do as well as I expected. I was always used to doing really good in school, and in high school, I mean, so it was kind of like—it felt—it made me feel like things weren't going right. And like /?/ happen to me, and it's like—it made me feel like, I guess I can say, stupid. I'm used to doing so good. What's happening? When I was in high school I always did really well—at least A's and B's. Last semester I ended up getting all A's and getting /?/ my final. So I guess I have that mentality where I would always do that way, do good, and I soon as I

came here and classes were harder. I tried my best and everything, but still. I am always the kind of person that I tried to push myself to get real good grades and doing my best....

Raul: How did you feel going into English 152?

Letty: I was disappointed, I'm like, like /?/ how if feel going backwards. I was used to moving forward and doing really well and I knew that 160 was basically where everybody started off. So it's like, great. I'm not even starting off /with/ everybody else. I'm going to a level back.

Letty, although not happy about her placement into Basic Writing, accepted her placement. She had, as Eleanor Kutz and Hephzibah Roskelly (1991) describe, accepted and internalized "the school culture's assessment of [her] abilities" although it made her feel that she was going "backwards" (p. 59). Being placed in Basic Writing and then struggling there is also what contributes heavily to her negative feeling about all her writing courses and about herself. This is clearly seen when she states:

> I was disappointed, I'm like, like /?/ how if feel going backwards. I was used to moving forward and doing really well, and I knew that 160 was basically where everybody started off. So it's like, great. I'm not even starting off /with/ everybody else. I'm going to a level back.

Juan

Juan's reaction to the class, on the other hand, was still quite different from that of Letty.[8] In fact, of the four focal students, he was the only one who enjoyed being in class as indicated by the following passage:

Pat: ...Everybody, what you need to have in your writing is everything that you notice about that ad, you put words on it. Got it? Got it? Got it? Understand? All right {clapping}. Thank you, thank you. Now I think we've done enough on uncovering of ads today. Are you kind of tired of uncovering ads?

Student: Yeah.

Juan: Let's go home.

Student 1: Is it okay if we talk about—

Pat: Juan, I thought you loved this class?

Juan: I do {Laughs}.

Pat: I thought that you, you just got depressed whenever—

Juan: I do, do that {laughs}.

Pat: That you lived for Monday, Wednesdays, Fridays. Okay. I gave. It's, it's a five page thing on starting to work on sentence combining. And I want,

> I want to start working on that. So I'd like, as I understand it, you don't have assignments in here because this stuff should all be done. So what I'd like to do is hand you out a uh sentence combining, and you don't need to do the whole thing, but the whole thing will be due in some point in time, so start working on it. And I'll tell you how far to get. The rest of you will be on call on Friday. We'll continue this process, and you'll come up here, and we'll do the same, same kind of thing. Uh, here's the first page.
>
> Student 2: Do you have any idea when the paper's going to be due?

As the passage shows, Juan not only enjoyed being in class, he excelled. Also, Juan functioned at a different level of abstract thinking from the other three focal students. As the next segment shows, many times throughout the course, when writing the essays, Juan deliberately and consciously went beyond Pat's and the class's expectations:

> Pat: {Two weeks before this session, Pat had asked the students to write an essay on an advertisement of their choosing. "Today" refers to that comment} some weeks ago, I handed out a, ditto on revision, practices. And they're on both sides, maybe six or seven of them. Would you find that piece of paper and take it out. It's called revision strategies. Looks like this, revision strategies. I'd like to use revision strategy one. And in a sense, this is probably the most exhaustive revision strategy. It really uncovers the structure of your writing. So we're using a comprehensive part, focused revision strategy. What I'd like to do is have the first person who is going to present come up and pass out the papers.

The students, after selecting an advertisement from a newspaper or magazine, were to describe the advertisement then tell why it worked. Thus, for the previous two weeks, this was what was happening. Each student was to present his/her essay to the class and explain why the ad works. For this class session, Juan read his essay exactly as he had written it:

> The American advertising medium exploits the American people's embedded freedom of choice rights to sell import products to them. At the same time these import buyers have some idea that every little dollar spent by them that leaves these this country, will continue to hurt the American economy.
>
> But the slap in the face about this sort of self indulging expressionism by American consumers is that the advertising medium as well as producers of expensive import products at time use the strongest icons America has (baseball in this case), to coaxed the foolish American consumer, and into betraying the American confidence. I, as well as anybody else knows, know

that one person buying one important car, stereo, television, watch, or whatever, will not hurt the economy. But let's look at the whole realistic picture. Let's take into account the billions of import products purchased by American on a annual basis. After we do that, let's imagine the billions of dollars that leave this country. Finally, let's look realistically at the American job market and the homeless trends, and try to figure out why many millions, many millions of Americans find themselves jobless and eventually homeless. It doesn't take a Nobel Prize winner in economy to figure that one out. While reflecting back to the content of the previous paragraph, keep in mind that almost all countries do not trade evenly with us. They import more products to our country, and they take in return as exports from ours.

This is how my ad reads. You'll find "Championship deals" during Tony Piet's World Series of Savings. "Tony Piet is swinging for the bleachers to bring you the best deals of the season, and A winning line up of America's best car and trucks. That's how the top of this particular ad reads, but with the image of what seems to be an American ball player hitting what seems to be, you guess it, a home run. This is of course followed by what seems to be special deals on American–Japanese cars. The ad doesn't tell you that you will be back stabbing your country's economy by buying that product. The ad doesn't tell you that these imposter imports, which they call American in the ad, are not really American. They're just accepted in American as Americans because so many middle /?/ Americans have made them acceptable, and even mainstream. So the advertising, the advertisers, dealers, and manufactures know that American are naive and callous enough to just want to buy a car regardless of where it's made and what adverse affects the purchase of one costs. These callous consumers really don't care where it was made or by whom. The ad doesn't ask you please forgive us for using the American pastime to sell imported products to the American public. We know that this exasperates the economy, the econ, the economic situation in America. But we don't care, and you probably don't care either. So just buy imported cars and products.

I know that Americans have tons of rights and freedoms. They're full of them, but sometimes Americans have to look beyond nitpicky constitutional freedoms that they so rightly possessed and analyze for themselves where exercising these rights is hurting America or not. This analyzing process takes little or no time, but it does require that one possess a heart towards ones less fortunate citizens. Let's be realistic. There's no question that import product buying is hurting America.

I know that the import product market is a big part of the American economy already, but if this country is going to improve any time soon, this part of the economy will need to be revised and rearrange to better suit the American companies so that they flourish and begin to hire Americans again. (The unemployment rate is somewhere near 10% as I write this). Let's keep in mind that legitimate research has shown that the impetus for joblessness,

> hopelessness, and increases in the crime rate is due to the craze that Americans have of buying whatever regardless of where it was made and who profit from its production of sales. Let's wise up, America. Let's stop reacting incorrectly to these ads selling import products and set the wheels in motion that will one day bring the American economy and the job market to life.

Juan has demonstrated in his writing what Pat has been wanting from all her students—essays that show abstract and logical thinking—the kind of thinking valued in our schools (Kutz and Roskelly, 1991, p. 45):

> Our school culture particularly values the ability to think and problem solve outside the context of one's own immediate experience, and to be self-reflective and aware of one's own thinking and ways of acting. And one aim of schooling in our society may be to facilitate these sorts of changes from thinking in personal, context–based terms to thinking more abstractly.... (p. 49)

As Kutz and Roskelly (1991) also stress, "More abstract thinking, in itself, is not always better" (p. 49). "Without rooting the abstract thoughts in the complex details of real life and real examples" the students will "become silenced" (pp. 49, 53). "The students will be reluctant to respond to the teacher's questions" for fear of "making mistakes" or they will revert to what they know (p. 53). And as the next segment shows, this is exactly what happened.

When Pat asked the students to respond to Juan's essay immediately after he finished reading the paper, the students avoided saying anything about the content, the main point of the paper, or even the structure. Rather, as the passage below shows, the focus was more on surface-level meaning:

> Pat: Uh, look up in your paper. What's Juan's bottom line?
> Letty: Don't buy imports.
> Pat: Yeah, Letty. You got it.
> Student 1: I thought Pontiac was an American product.
> Juan. No, but there's Nissan, I guess.
> Student 1: Oh.
> Juan: But they're saying uh, "America's cars."
> Student 1: Oh.
> Juan: Like they're made in America.
> Student 1: That's where I got a little confused because I thought Pontiac was

an American-made car—

Juan: It is.

Student 1: Yeah, I know, and that's why—

Juan: That's another—

Student 1: I know maybe—

Juan: I didn't explain but I did say that. You know. And special deals on American and Japanese cars.

Student 1: Yeah, oh.

Juan: It's after the second paragraph.

Pat: Any other questions about it?

Student 2: Only like in the middle of the paragraph it says, "After we do that /lets imagine"/.

Juan: On what paragraph?

Student 2: First page.

Juan: Okay.

Student 2: Like, in the middle of the paragraph.

Juan: Okay, "What's affecting."

Student 1: It's about /?/.

Juan: Okay, after we do that "Lets imagine the—" Okay I'm just saying—

Student 2: No, no–no, "After we do that."

Juan: After we do that "Lets imagine the," Oh after that?

Student 3: "After we do that" comma, "Let's imagine—

Juan: Okay. Okay, all right yeah. Do you understand what I'm saying there?

Student 2: Yeah. I'm just saying that—

Juan: I thought you were trying to ask me to clarify what—

Student 2: Oh, okay.

Juan: I meant, you know.

Pat: Okay. No, that's good. That's good, and you read it, if we could tell, especially if you needed a comma because, you know, when we talk—

Student: We don't—

Pat: When we talk, you know there is a comma talalalalalal. Now there another, there's another sentence in that paragraph where you need a comma for that same rule—

Juan: Oh, yeah—

Pat: Student 2, find it!

Student 2: I don't know.

Pat: Pull up Student 3 next to you and see if she can help you out. Or anybody? There's another one.

Connie: Here's one, and "finally?"

Pat: What Connie?

Connie: And "finally" probably.

Pat: That wouldn't be bad. Where is that? But I didn't but I–

Connie: Go to the next sentence. After—

Pat: "And finally," you could put a comma there. Okay what you want to do

is a major pause, but grammatically you don't have to. That would be fine, Connie. It would not be wrong. I want ungrammatically—
Student 3: Where it says. Where it says "By reflecting back on what you have just read about"—
Letty: Yeah.
Pat: Comma, yes. "By reflecting back on what you have just read" comma.
Student 2: Let's see. I think I see another one of those by the second sentence.
Letty: "At the same time."
Student 2: "At the same time."
Juan: Is that clear? That last sentence in the first paragraph. They import—
Connie: Shouldn't there be a transition some, somewhere in there? Like, into the next paragraph about the ad? There's no transitional sentence.
Juan: I wanted to start right off with the bat. I didn't want a say "this is how the ad really intended." I figured that if I did it in bold like that, that everybody would figure out this is the ad. This is one of the ads that I'm talking about. So I thought that was a transition in itself.
Student: How did you get the cool little arrow?

Instead of the students focusing on Juan's ideas, we see Student 1 focus on what he knows, which is to identify mistakes. Thus, Student 1 focuses on Juan being unclear about what an American-made car is and what is not:

Pat: Uh, look up in your paper. What's Juan's bottom line?
Letty: Don't buy imports.
Pat: Yeah, Letty. You got it.
Student 1: I thought Pontiac was an American product.
Juan. No, but there's Nissan, I guess.
Student 1: Oh.
Juan: But they're saying uh, "America's cars."
Student 1: Oh.
Juan: Like they're made in America.
Student 1: That's where I got a little confused because I thought Pontiac was an American-made car—
Juan: It is.
Student 1: Yeah, I know, and that's why—
Juan: That's another—
Student 1: I know maybe—
Juan: I didn't explain but I did say that. You know. And special deals on American and Japanese cars.
Student 1: Yeah, oh.

As another example of focusing on the negative, there is question about punctuation:

Pat: Okay. No, that's good. That's good, and you read it, if we could tell, especially if you needed a comma because, you know, when we talk—
Student: We don't—
Pat: When we talk, you know there is a comma talalalalalal. Now there another, there's another sentence in that paragraph where you need a comma for that same rule—
Juan: Oh, yeah—
Pat: Student 2, find it!
Student 2: I don't know.
Pat: Pull up Student 3 next to you and see if she can help you out. Or anybody? There's another one.

Finally, there is also a question about the lack of transitions:

Connie: Shouldn't there be a transition some, somewhere in there? Like, into the next paragraph about the ad? There's no transitional sentence.
Juan: I wanted to start right off with the bat. I didn't want a say "this is how the ad really intended." I figured that if I did it in bold like that, that everybody would figure out this is the ad. This is one of the ads that I'm talking about. So I thought that was a transition in itself.

The discussion ends with a student making a comment on Juan's use of a graphical symbol. The real purpose for Juan presenting his essays is avoided.

Conclusion

The feelings that Letty and Connie had about writing and about themselves are not unique to them. These are very common among many Latino students (and many other minority students as well). In both students, I saw frustrations—the anger, the suspicions, and the mistrust I have seen in many Latino students—that I have felt myself. These students do feel that school is trying to change them and the price of that change is too high (Ogbu, 1991; Valverde, 1987). Many feel that maybe there is something wrong with them, but no one in the school is willing to tell them what that something is. Thus, many students (like Joe) feel that their only option is to stop and dropout. Joe is not alone in this phenomenon. This is a phenomenon distinctive to Latino students—differing from, for example, white, working-class students' learning from a white, middle–class teacher (Ybarra, 2001, p.46). "What continues to happen to many students like Joe is that they continue to drop out in record numbers. Too many Latinos like Joe withdraw from Basic Writing and even more disturbing, drop out of college in record numbers" (Ybarra, 2001, p. 46).

Although Juan is successful, not just in this class, but in all his work, he still has a deep mistrust for the class, the instructor, and other students. We can see this in his essay. He dis–identifies from the American culture. He uses words like "foolish," "naive," and "callous" to identify American society. As Juan states, they "backstab" their own economy, creating joblessness and homelessness. They don't care about the effects of their behavior. He spreads this dis-identification, his sense of superiority, to his classmates and to the teacher when he writes, "You probably don't care either." Like Connie and Joe, Juan indicates that he does not identify with "real" American culture. And like Connie, and presumably Joe, Juan does not identify with the Latino culture either.

Allowing her initial question about "Juan's bottom line" to degenerate into irrelevant trivia, Pat may be reflecting the same inability to understand Juan for who he is that she articulated toward Connie and Joe, and implied to Letty. Teachers, and the larger culture they represent, can make it impossible for Latinos to feel at home in the classroom.

The confusion and anger Latino students have about composition and English courses results from how and what we teach beyond writing skills; they result from how we (as instructors) treat students in Basic Writing courses. We work on fixing their punctuation problems, their grammar problems, and their language interference problems; we assign worksheets; we ask for countless rewrites; we work on editing. After all the help we give these students, we see only some progress in the students' understanding of how to write an academic paper. The students continue to have the same problems paper after paper, even after completing Basic Writing, and assume that they are not very bright or intelligent.

I contend that as teachers of writing we do not always know what is expected from "minority" students—particularity in Basic Writing. Consequently, we do not understand the differences students bring with them. As a result, we see the problems students have in their writing as that, just writing issues. Because these students are not able to overcome their writing problems even after all the help we have given them, we tend to see them as not very intelligent. This supports Bloome's (1989) argument that "[s]tudents whose linguistic and interactional behavior" when associated with minority cultures is "often viewed as lacking skills to participate in high status literacy activities" (p. 19). We then, as Luis Moll (1988) contends, unconsciously (or purposely) "water down the curriculum" (p. 102). Or we interpret the defensive posturing of these Latino students as not wanting to be in the class, not interested in learning to write, not interested in being in college, even as hostile. So we find ways to help the student withdraw, drop.

Angela Valenzuela (1999) rightly argues that many students, particularly United States–born youth, do not necessarily oppose school; "[t]hey oppose a schooling process that disrespects them; they oppose not education, but schooling" (p. 5). They oppose how education "is offered to them" (p.19). Valenzuela refers to this process as "subtractive schooling"—a process by which school creates "social, linguistic, and cultural divisions among the students and between the students and [teachers]...to the extent that relationships with teachers affect students' schooling orientations and achievement" (pp.5, 30).

The result is that we end up with students who are suspicious and angry. They do not oppose school. They oppose "a schooling process that disrespects them and formally and informally...[and] fractures students' cultural and ethnic identities, creating social, linguistic, and social division among the students and between the teacher and the staff" (Valenzuela, 1999, p.5). These students feel disaffiliated from school and distance themselves even more. Thus, our job as teachers and researchers is to continue to understand the differences, the cultural identities of our students, and to develop strategies that will help students and teachers build "bridges" between these differences that will help students become part of the school and not feel disaffiliated from it.

Notes

1. All the names of the students and instructor have been changed.
2. A suburb of Chicago.
3. It is in the release forms where I asked the students to identify themselves ethnically.
4. For a copy of her essay, see Appendix C, Connie's Essay.
5. Here again, Pat asked me to turn off my tape recorder.
6. This is a very similar response to my reaction when I took Basic Writing. See Chapter 1, "My Story–As Example."
7. I made several attempts to contact him at home, but I got no response to the messages or letters I sent him.
8. Although Juan sat on the same side of the classroom as Letty, Connie, and Joe, I cannot recall seeing him talk to any of them.

CHAPTER 4

What is to be Learned

> Educators and policymakers must pay close attention to how our educational policies and programs meet the needs of our students from diverse linguistic and cultural backgrounds. More often than not, both formal and informal school policies discourage the use of Spanish in the classroom and make no attempt to welcome the Latino community within the school setting.... In order to foster social justice schools need to be culturally sensitive, work towards abolishing stereotypes, and provide Latino students with opportunities to learn about their diverse histories.
>
> —Nancy López , 2004, pp. 358,359

Introduction

In Chapter 1, I used my own personal experiences both as a student and as an instructor to better understand the Latino students in my classes. My willingness to reflect on my own position and engage in introspection, although unusual in academe, is deserving of recognition. My documenting my own history has allowed me to analyze how the academe has influenced my own thinking, values, and ways of being. I make clear that these influences are both negative and positive. By discussing openly my decreasing proficiency in Spanish, my distancing from the Latino community, and my struggles in understanding how to write, I uncover a very real desire to think deeply about the problems now facing the current generation of Latino students. Through my own experiences I show that the prevalence of failure among "Latino students in particular Basic Writing courses suggest a (dis)connection between the cultural backgrounds and corresponding thought processes of Latino students in the learning environment in the composition classroom" (Ybarra, 2001, p. 38).

In Chapter 2, I focused on the cultural schemata of academic discourse of a writing classroom to show why academic writing is a difficult task for many minority students, and in particular Latino students. Students who are not part of the mainstream, particularly Latino students, not only see this pattern as confusing, but also as a hostile attempt to change who they are. This process of change produces epistemological violence to Latino students of tracking because of the marginalizing and cultural implications that take place.

Accordingly, here is where we see that, although the instructor has a broad understanding of essayist literacy, she has a somewhat ineffective interpretation of it. The instructor ultimately reduces teaching to a tripartite model. While some students are familiar and comfortable with academic discourse and excel in writing courses, others are not so familiar with this writing style and are even resistant to learning it.

In Chapter 3, I suggest and argue that the suspicion and anger felt by each of the four Latino students come from what schools are teaching. When schools attempt to teach students from different cultures how to generate written language, they are in fact teaching them how to become “white.” As Farr (1986) states, "When students 'shift toward the standard' and learn to write, they are learning mainstream features" (p. 35). This is what they, many Latino students, are resisting, i.e., becoming enculturated. The degrees of resistance vary because of the difference in cultures: “Different cultural models provoke different behaviors” (Ogbu, 1991, p. 7). Although each of the four Latino students’ reactions varied, the students do have something in common. All four Latino students responded negatively and suspiciously to what was being taught to them.

Despite numerous studies attributing socioeconomic and cultural origins to this phenomenon, the actual reality of this ethnic/racial division is staggering. All the more discouraging is the fact that this ethnic division of basic and regular composition courses doesn’t appear to have changed through the years (Ybarra, 2001, p. 38). It is interesting to note that, while I was a graduate student at the University of Illinois, Latinos comprised 10.1 percent of the undergraduate student population, yet Latinos made up 26 percent of students enrolled in Basic Writing (UIC, 1994). Several questions come into view when analyzing placement patterns in Basic Writing courses. Why are Latino students placed in larger numbers in Basic Writing courses than other groups in composition courses? Equally puzzling is why do these students not matriculate into the credit–bearing courses in numbers that reflect their distribution in the university?

Understanding why Latino students do poorly in writing courses is becoming an ever–more important issue because Latinos are the fastest growing group in the United States. With the increasing Latino population, one would assume that we would see a corresponding increase in Latino college completion rates, but unfortunately the opposite is true (Ybarra, 2001, p. 38). While we do see more Latino students entering college, current census data show that the retention rate for Latinos at all levels of schooling remains low. As stated by Gabriella Gonzalez (2004): "Unfortunately, Latino students as a group have a higher dropout rate than any other minority subgroup population in our schools, and this rate is growing.... The overall high school graduation rate of 53 percent is the lowest of all major ethnic groups in the Unites States, (p. 235)." Additionally, as argued by Raul Ybarra (2001) "the statistics do not identify or apparently explain the problem of the disproportionate placement of Latino students in Basic Writing and their limited success in producing acceptable academic writing" (p. 38). Additionally, considering that many Latinos after twelve years of schooling apparently fail to perform at the levels expected of them, how does placement in Basic Writing courses affect Latino students even beyond factors such as individual self-esteem?

In this book, I proposed a framework that places the means to understanding this model on how the communication is patterned and organized and also how communication in one particular community interacts with all the other speech communities. This framework also provides a basis for evaluating communication patterns and communication breakdowns in a classroom setting and shows that communication breakdowns because of cultural differences do contribute to the poor performance of Latino students and other minority students in composition classes at the college level. However, instead of creating bridges to overcome the differences, many schools dismiss these breakdowns as students not wanting to be in the classroom or as students being lazy or hostile and thereby silencing the student point of view. Exposing the larger hidden curriculum of assimilation, or Anglo/middle class conformity, allows me to focus on the constraints placed on students.

To show a specific example of these constraints—this (dis)connection, this cultural dissonance—I come back to a discussion I had with the student who was instrumental in helping me narrow my topic for this book, Mari. Mari was not a student of the class I have described. Rather, Mari was a student who took one of my Basic Writing courses two years earlier and did very well. The conversation took place after Mari had completed two writing courses with me (the Basic Writing and the regular composition course) and was enrolled in a third, the research composition course, with another instructor. I asked her what she thought of the Basic Writing class. This was her response:

Raul: About my class, what did you not like about it?

Mari: As I told you, /this class/ here I didn't want to go to your class every morning…because I didn't want to talk in class; I didn't want to. I didn't like that.

When she said "because I didn't want to talk in class," I knew that she did not want to talk because she was scared—scared of my finding out that she was not very bright, that she did not belong, or that I was going to embarrass her (Kutz and Roskelly, 1991, p. 53). What I remember about Mari is that she did speak in my class, but it took much encouragement, prodding, and nudging to get her to feel comfortable enough to talk and to question.

In my class, as suggested by Eleanor Kutz, Suzy Groden, and Vivian Zamel in *The Discovery of Competence: Teaching and Learning with Diverse Student Writers* (1993), Mari was in an environment that encouraged her to use writing to make sense of the world around her, to learn, to conceptualize, to inquire, and then to communicate this sense to herself and to others (p. 31). She was provided with opportunities to use language in multiple ways so that she could use her writing, reading, and speaking voices "[t]o speak with an authority" that revealed the self-assured person I knew she could be (p. 31). By the end of the semester, Mari was talking. She was quite successful at speaking out and at questioning. Furthermore, she saw the importance and value of speaking in class, as she said in our conversation:

Mari: …Now I understand that it's good to help you to decide to work on your own…what areas to work, and that's what I need the most. . . . I like it—maybe it's—because the—it's really different to make me feel good, to give me confidence.

Then Mari told me about her research composition class and the instructor and when she did speak in class—when she did question—how the instructor made her feel:

Raul: Okay, you did average work for Comp. 101, how do you feel about Comp. 101?

Mari: 101 I didn't like. I didn't like it because we got definite assignments, awful. I didn't like that.

Raul: Who was your instructor?

Mari: He is student also, B.

Raul: B?

Mari: Yeah. One day I said to him, I don't like this class because of this, this, and this. And he got upset, and he said, because I was criticizing him, but

> I—I did not expect that reaction from him—so—Oh my God. Maybe I'll get a final hard or something.

With the "Oh my God," I saw the fear come back again—this fear and suspicion of anticipating more or harder work because of what she thought was speaking out against the instructor. Somewhere along her education, she has learned to equate speaking with being punished (Walsh, 1991, pp. 43, 47). Mari had in fact "internalized through interpretation" what she had been taught and told as well as what she had experienced "to regard education with mistrust" and suspicion (Walsh, 1991, p. 47; Kutz and Roskelly, 1991, p. 53).

In addition, this conversation only seemed to confirm her belief that something was wrong with her. I wondered why. More importantly, I had to ask why she came to me rather than to her current instructor:

> Mari: Because we trust you more than him. That's why I bring my papers to you.

The words "I trust you more than him" stood out because of the double meaning I got from them. In one aspect, Mari trusted me enough to confide in me that she was struggling and that she was fearful of the possibility of showing me that she was not bright or intelligent enough. She showed this by continuing to come to me for help although she was no longer a student of mine. However, Mari also said "we trust you more then him" and I took this to mean that she also did not trust me—at least not completely. Therefore, I had to ask why. This was her response:

> Mari: That's how, that how I am. Plus, all these things we have, you know. We're learning, the teachers have told us that's wrong. It's like, wait a minute, you know, you could trust a teacher to a point 'cause other teachers have told us, and we don't know who to trust. I mean, we trust you, you know, but....

At that moment of this realization, I realized that I too am looked on suspiciously even though I too am Latino. Yet, it is within this context that I understand why many Latinos are suspicious and have problems when they enter a writing course at the college level—why I am a person they also cannot trust. Because I have associated with the white mainstream culture for so long, I have internalized many white mainstream cultural characteristics. Consequently, many Latinos not only feel that I have assimilated with the white culture; they feel that I am no longer a person of color. I have succeeded in becoming a member of the academic community. But at what cost? To answer this question, I looked at what I had left behind.

I see myself far removed from my own culture. I have very little contact with the Latino community and I now struggle with my first language, Spanish. Although, both as her professor and as a fellow Latino, I was hurt at not being trusted by Mari, I understood her fears because I share the same suspicions—many of same fears. In one of my many discussions with my adviser Professor Marcia Farr, she suggested that the problems I had, and that many other Latinos struggled with, was not just a problem with learning to write. Rather, the problems have more to do with language, with family, and the culture of the students and that often these cultures were different from that of the school (Farr, 1986, p. 200). It was this conversation with my adviser that ultimately led me to write this book. I thought about whether I had gone through a cultural transformation. I did not think I had at first, but as I progressed through the first chapter, I was forced to step back and think about who I was and where I was. I realized I had gone through a cultural transformation.

When I first started kindergarten, I was held back because I could not speak English. In the third grade, I was almost held back again because I could not write very well. In junior high school and high school, I could not move beyond remedial classes in English. As I progressed through high school, I spoke with little or no Spanish accent when I spoke English, but I did have an accent when I spoke Spanish. I would switch from Spanish to English when I could not think of the word in Spanish. When I decided that I was going to do whatever I needed to do to pass Basic Writing, I passed. This was a crucial point in my cultural transformation. Since then, my grade point average went from a C average to an A average; I have received my bachelor's degree in Plant Science and a master's in English Composition, both fields dominated by Anglos. Then I entered the Ph.D. program in English, a field of study that is predominantly Anglo as well.

As the excerpt from the conversation just related, Mari was very suspicious about writing, about the writing course she was taking, the instructors teaching this course, and of me. Even though Mari had successfully completed basic writing with an A, her struggle with writing did not stop. In my many discussions with Mari I found that she had, somewhere along in her education, learned to equate speaking out with getting punished, and that "her teacher's voice," her current writing instructor's voice, was "the only one to listen to" (Walsh, 1991, pp. 43, 44; hooks, 1994, p. 150). More importantly, Mari perceived that I had given her the wrong information by getting her to voice her opinion, and because of this, she was now in trouble with her current writing instructor, but she could not say anything to her current writing instructor or to me because of what she understood of the unequal teacher/student relationship.

This is a similar reaction, this fear that Lourdes Diaz Soto (1997) describes in her observation: "Their future appeared to dim as their voices continued to be disregarded and the fear (miedo)…crept into many hearts" (p. 64). Or as Kutz and Roskelly (1991) stress "Without rooting the abstract thoughts in the complex details of real life and real examples [the students will] become silenced. The students will be reluctant to respond to the teacher's questions for fear of making mistakes," or they will revert to what they know (pp. 49, 53). Nancy López is even more direct and refers to this distancing as a "silencing process." And this process has a devastating effect on the student. As López writes, "[s]ilencing the cultural background of Latino students is a form of academic violence, which may lead them to feel that their culture is deficient" (López, 2004, 359). The instructor then has successfully reduced teaching to "a narrowly defined concern with instrumental techniques, skills, and objectives" (Giroux, 1992, p. 98). But is this all there is to learning how to write—memorizing the rules of academic discourse?

Obviously, the answer is NO! For if this were the case, then we wouldn't have what Patricia Bizzell (1986) describes as discrepancies in helping students to successfully complete composition courses. She points out that while some students are familiar and comfortable with academic discourse and excel in writing courses, others are not so familiar with this writing style and are even resistant to learning it. How well and easily students learn this model depends on who the students are and where they come from. Marcia Farr and Harvey Daniels (1986) further state that when "Western schools attempt to teach students how to generate written language that displays these qualities [like] objectivity and explicitness" (p. 31), this is what it means to become literate in school, which translates into becoming successful in our society. When a student does not demonstrate these features, s/he is labeled as having something wrong, and that "wrong" must be fixed. They are then placed in Basic Writing not so much to learn to write, but to understand the structure of writing (Ybarra, 2000).

Is this what happened to Connie, Letty, Joe, and Juan? I say yes. I suggest that the anger Latino students have about writing and English courses results from how we teach beyond writing skills; the anger results from how we as instructors treat students in writing courses—that they are not very bright or intelligent. As a result, we unconsciously (or purposely) "water down the curriculum" (Moll, 1988). Paulo Friere (1997) in *Pedagogy of the Oppressed* supports my answer. Friere is critical of mainstream teaching practices, referring to mainstream education as "banking education." According to Friere, in the banking approach to education the teacher deposits information into an empty account because the "teacher knows, the students do not know" (Rivera, 2001, p. 37). "Education thus becomes an act of depositing, in which the students are depositories and the teacher is the depositor, instead of communicating, the teacher issues communiqués and makes deposits which the students patiently receive, memorize, and repeat" (p. 53). In this atmosphere, the student is seen as an object and is submersed in a "culture of silence," resulting in the student feeling powerless because of his or her inability to change his or her life (p. 53).

Letty is such an example. She increasingly became more silent as the semester progressed. Her silence alienated her from the classroom even more as she experienced "repeated failure and repeated negative encounters with her teacher" (Erickson, 1996, p. 41). Consequently, as a defensive mechanism and "not necessarily within full reflective awareness," Letty's silence is because of her conflict with the process of her learning to write and this conflict is shown as an oppositional pattern, her "symbol of her disaffiliation with what she experienced" (p. 41).

Accounting for Latino Students' Mistrust

Although the answer above explains why Mari reacted the way she did to her instructor's comments, it does not explain how and why Mari learned to react this way, that cultural and communication differences played a part in Mari's response and reaction. For example, as Farr (1986) points out in her article, "Language, Culture and Writing," many of these students, "have spent up to [twelve] years in a context in which the standard is taught, or at least used and modeled," and we have promised to prepare them for college (p. 201). But then as Mike Rose (1988a) points out in much of his research, when students like Mari enter college, many of these same Latino students are placed in Basic Writing courses where they are labeled "marginal," "high risk," or "at risk." However, these students do not understand why they are put in these classes, so they ask us. And as many noted composition scholars have suggested in their research, we don't tell them. We don't tell because we don't really understand why they are having difficulty. So many of these students come up with their own conclusions that maybe something is wrong with them; that they're really not bright enough; that they will never understand writing this academic discourse. All this adds to their frustration and anger. Thus, it is not surprising that Mari felt that she was not bright or intelligent enough, that she did not belong, and that she couldn't trust anyone—including me.

These feelings that Mari had about writing and about herself are not unique to her. This is very common among many Latino students (and many other minority students as well). For example, in all four Latino students I described in Chapter 3—Connie, Letty, Joe, and Juan—I saw the frustrations, the anger, the suspicions, and the mistrust I have seen in many Latino students. All four Latino students were caught between school culture and home culture and struggled with their own identities. The instructor further contributed to these students' struggles by not understanding who these students were or where they come from.

As demonstrated with Letty, what continues to happen to many of these students is that their struggle with writing does not stop even though they may have successfully completed the Basic Writing course. The tensions of being frightened, confused, and angry are still there. The tensions are compounded because these students don't understand why they are having so much difficulty with writing. They don't and can't understand why they have so many mistakes in their essays. As David Bartholomae (1988b), Mina Shaughnessy (1977), and Mike Rose (1989) all suggest in their research, many of these students feel as though something is wrong with them, but no one is willing to tell them what that is. Being placed in Basic Writing for many of these Latino students only reinforces the idea that they are not good enough to enter the required composition course, and this adds to the suspicions many Latino students have towards mainstream culture and vice versa (Ogbu, 1987; Valverde, 1987; Jacob and Jordan, 1996). Many feel that their only option is to stop and to drop out.

John Ogbu argues that the reason for the negative reaction and for the differences in the reaction of each Latino student is not as much the differences in culture but the way in which the schools are structured that lead to the deep mistrust (D'Amato, 1993, p. 185, Ogbu, 1993, p. 241). Ogbu (1987) writes about how many schools perceive ethnic students as having low levels of intelligence because of linguistic and cultural differences and thus place such students in remedial courses. Fedrick Erickson (1996) supports this claim when he notes that many educators make assumptions about the students' performance based on poor attitudes about school. Moreover, many educators "assume that a [student's] level of...proficiency in English indicates a similar level of proficiency in reading and writing" (Moll, 1988, p. 102). "This occurs when teachers explicitly display marked differences in expectations for levels of academic achievement they hold for students" (p. 3). The result then is the "watering down" of the curriculum to accommodate these students (Moll, 1986, p. 102). Louis Mirón (1997) refers to this as "academic discrimination" hidden in the curriculum (pp. 3, 5).

Latino students (and many other minority students), by the time they get to college, have repeatedly been faced with being seen as unintelligent, or as low achievers (Erickson, 1993, p. 41). Susan Philips (1983) provides an example of how the differences in discourse patterns, due to structural and cultural differences, affect learning in her study of the Warm Spring Indians. The teachers perceived the Indians as shy, as not responsive, and as unable to comprehend when it came to talking because of the lack of responses in certain classroom situations like "Show and Tell." However, as Philips' ethnographic study shows, none of the three descriptive traits, shyness, non responsiveness, and lack of comprehension, were accurate. The problems the children were having were traced to differences between the children's home culture and the school culture. The problem is that the Indian children withdrew from classroom interaction because it required them to behave in ways that were not appropriate in their communities. Although the students were responding to the structural differences of the Anglo-mainstream instructors, it was the differences in culture that affected the communication between the teachers and the students.

As these students grow older "and experience repeated failure and repeated negative encounters" with teachers, instead of developing patterns that are consistent "with the dominant culture, they develop oppositional cultural patterns," similar to what happened to Connie when Pat interpreted Connie's frustrations as hostility toward her (Erickson, 1993, pp. 45, 46).[1] Moreover, these student see school as trying to change them, but the personal costs of learning to become members of the school culture are too high (Farr and Daniels, 1986; Ogbu, 1990). As a result, many of these students choose to fail or reject school either outright like Joe, or subtly like Letty.

On average, not only do involuntary minorities have far more trouble with their teachers, they have a more "difficult time respecting their teachers and learning from them" than mainstream students. They also have a much more difficult time with their own identities (Gibson, 1996, p. 366). Involuntary minorities (such as African Americans, Puerto Ricans, and some Mexicans) are those who did not have a choice. They are in the United States by force or through colonization. They see many of the barriers—economic, social, and political—as oppressive: "They are less able than the immigrant to overcome [these cultural/language] problems and therefore tend to experience a greater degree of social adjustment" (Ogbu, 1987, p. 147). These "greater degree[s] of social adjustment" can have a negative effect on the students, which could account for the "persistent high rate of school failure" (Ogbu, 1990, p. 92). Mirón (1997) supports this claim when he writes, "The worst possibility is that low academic expectations for poor minority youth leads to their...dropping out of school" (p. 3).

Voluntary minorities are those ethnic groups that came to the United States of their own choosing (Ogbu, 1990, p. 92). They came here to make a better life for themselves (for example, some Asians, some Mexicans, many Latin Americans).[2] Ogbu (1991) further notes that voluntary "minorities are more willing than involuntary minorities to accommodate themselves to school rules" (p. 4). These voluntary groups do not see discrimination necessarily as bad because it may not be as severe as it was in their homeland:

> For this reason, the immigrants see the cultural differences as barriers to be overcome in order to achieve their long-range goals of future employment. . . .They therefore do not perceive or interpret learning the cultural features of the schools required for social adjustment and academic performance as threatening to their own culture, language, and identity. (Ogbu, 1990, p. 92)

Thus, "immigrant minorities or those with an immigrant orientation have an easier time excelling in school" (Ogbu, 1996, p. 157). They see learning to write as a "barrier to overcome" (Ogbu, 1990, p. 157); they see "learning the English language and adjusting to the standard practices of school" important "in order to achieve his [or her] goal" (Ogbu, 1991, p. 157). We can see this idea supported by Juan himself in a discussion he had with the instructor about one of the writing topics assigned (the topic is on issues of conformity):

> Pat: Is life always one of conformity? Then...we got to redefine what conformity is the way we were talking about it. I mean, could you say that I conform because the sun rises at six a.m., so I wake up? And I

conform just because the night comes, and I go to sleep? Is that conformity? Now if we are to take that as conformity, than what is conformity? We got to look at the, what we are talking about. How is peer pressure different from the sun rising and the bell ringing?

Juan: The degree, the different degrees of conformity. There are some that are so second nature that's not conforming anymore. It's second nature. Then there's degrees of conformity that can affect you big time.

Pat: Affect you big time?

Juan: Yeah.

Pat: Like what?

Juan: Like being what we're just talking about, being here. I mean nobody has to be here, but they choose to be here because they want to move forward. They want to move ahead. They want to progress.

At first glance, Juan's participation seems to follow Ogbu's (1993) theoretical concept, that students who are born in another country (voluntary minorities) tend to do better and are less likely to drop out from school than involuntary minorities (p. 87). Moreover, involuntary minorities have a "deeper mistrust" than voluntary minority (as Connie's, Letty's, and Joe's lack of participation demonstrate). Because voluntary minorities choose to be here, they are less resistant; they see the value of schooling—to get ahead. They "see acculturation in an 'additive' rather than a 'subtractive' light" (Gibson, 1991, p. 367). And "teachers, by and large, like teaching immigrant students" because these students have this sense of purpose and direction (Gibson, 1991, p. 362).

It is here where Ogbu's concept cannot account for Juan's mistrust. As Erickson (1993) notes that although Ogbu's

> Explanation can account for the school success of immigrant minority students in school, it does not account for the success of domestic minority students, whether the conditions of that school success involve culturally responsive pedagogy or not. (p. 35)

Erickson goes on to write that "enough exceptions to the general pattern can be found so as to raise serious questions about the adequacy of [Ogbu's] explanation as it has been articulated presently" (p. 35). This is supported by other scholars such as John D'Amato: "the caste like minority position is unable to explain why the children of caste like minorities do not always reject their teachers" (D'Amato, 1993, p. 187). And Philips (1983): "failure" does not come about because these children are members of an involuntary ethnic group and have developed a psychological orientation toward schooling which prevent themselves from succeeding (p. xvii). We can also argue that Ogbu's theory cannot account for Connie's and Letty's success with Basic Writing and beyond either. Erickson (1993) goes on to argue that the differences in behavior, attitude, and mistrust are not just "a simple matter of mis-communication" caused by differences in structural differences (p. 41). The problem is much more complex. The "lack of understanding could well originate in the cultural and linguistic dissonance that arises between Latino students discourse patterns used by most Latino students and academic patterns of writing" (Ybarra, 2001, p. 48). It is most likely that Latino student resistance comes from this lack of understanding, which researchers have not yet explored.

In the particular Basic Writing class I describe in this book, what the instructor did here was what she had been consciously doing all semester (purposely at times and unconsciously at others) reinforcing the cultural model of academic discourse—essayist literacy. Although understanding the parts are important when writing, as many scholars have pointed out for many years, writing is much, much more. "Teaching this culturally dominant structure to Latino students accounts for the assessment of their work as problematic in many writing courses because many Latinos don't think in this tripartite structure" (Ybarra, 2001, p. 48). The required tripartite structure conflicts with the oral discourse patterns, which are influenced by Spanish syntax, discourse rules, and cadence (Ybarra, 1997, 2001). As D. R. Randell argues, "When Anglo instructors ask [Latino] students to state their thesis at the beginning of the essay, they're asking students to go against their culture…." (1998, p. 33). This is further compounded because we as teachers are going to evaluate how well these students write. Further compounding this matter shows that students also don't understand what we are teaching nor why we are teaching writing this way "despite the fact that they [may] have spent up to [twelve] years in a context in which the standard taught" (Farr, 1986, p.201). Moreover, Latino students see school as trying to change them, but the personal costs of learning to become members of the school culture are often too high (Farr and Daniels, 1986, Ogbu, 1990).

As a result, many of these students choose to reject school and choose to fail. This is what they, the many Latino students, are resisting—becoming enculturated. Students, especially those from ethnic groups that are repeatedly discriminated against in society, such as Latino students who have experienced marginalization in twelve years of previous schooling, will see this as a hostile act and resist learning. Teaching to this structural schema suggests a rationale for the pervasiveness and functions of this structure in education, especially when teaching to minority, in this case Latino, students. As shown in Chapter 3, the degrees of resistance vary because of the differences in cultures between the students. "Different cultural models provoke different behaviors, and on the instructor's own understanding of what he or she is teaching" (Ogbu, 1991, p. 7). Where the students come from in terms of family, culture, and education plays a crucial role in how the students are going to react to the Basic Writing course. These factors also influence the adaptation patterns to the school of the individual student (Gibson, 1996, p. 113, Ogbu, 1991, p. 4). As Ogbu (1991) writes:

> Recent ethnographic studies...indicate, specifically, that there may be different patterns of adaptation in schools which lead to different school success for immigrant and nonimmigrant minorities, partly because of different historical experiences which lead to different adaptive responses. (p. 4)

Ogbu theorizes that the problem with many Latino students is the "deep mistrust" they have for schools (1991, p. 28). He writes about the alienation and mistrust that many non mainstream groups have for the mainstream culture and its institutions and about the "past discriminatory educational policies and practices" such as stereotyping, tracking, and labeling (1987, p. 154). We promise to prepare them for college, but then, as Rose (1988b) argues many of these same Latino students are placed in Basic Writing courses where they are labeled "marginal, 'high risk,' or 'at risk'" and continue to struggle" (p. 2). This is so "despite the fact that they have spent up to [twelve] years in a context in which the standard is taught, or at least used and modeled" (Farr, 1986, p. 201). The American Council on Education supports Farr: "Native U.S. students continue to make up more than one-half of the students in these [remedial] courses" (Knopp, 1995, p. 8). However, while the resistance framework charts minority student failure in terms of oppositional identities and resistant stances, as further argued by such scholars Min-Zhan Lu, Henry Giroux, and others, it does not fully explain the four Latino students' reactions.

Valenzuela (1999) argues that many students, particularly United States–born youth, do not necessarily oppose school; "They oppose a schooling process that disrespects them; they oppose not education, but schooling" (p. 5). They oppose how education "is offered to them" (p. 19). Valenzuela refers to this process as "subtractive schooling" (p. 5), a process by which school creates "social, linguistic, and cultural divisions among the students and between the students and [teachers] to the extent that relationships with teachers affect students' schooling orientations and achievement" (pp. 5, 30). The result is that we end up with students who are suspicious and angry. They feel disaffiliated from school. Thus, they distance themselves even more. As Erickson (1993) describes:

> The more alienated the students become, the less they persist in doing schoolwork. Thus they fall farther and farther behind in academic achievement. The student becomes either actively resistant—seen as salient and incorrigible—or passively resistant—fading into the woodwork as an anonymous well-behaved, low achieving student. (p. 41)

Furthermore, as Bartholomae (1988b), Shaughnessy (1977), and Rose (1989) all suggest in their research, many of these students feel as though something is wrong with them, but no one is willing to tell them what that is. Being placed in Basic Writing, for many of these Latino students, only reinforces the idea that they are not good enough to enter the required composition course, and this adds to the suspicions many Latino students already have toward mainstream culture and vice versa (Ogbu, 1993a, 1993b, 1991, 1990; Valverde, 1987; Jacob and Jordan, 1996).

To add to these differences and complexities, as Juan demonstrated, not all minority students reject the school culture (Farr, 1986; Ogbu, 1990). Juan was the only one of the four who seemed to have enjoyed being in the class. He was the only one of the four who excelled.

Concluding Thoughts

I have and will continue to teach other courses besides Basic Writing, but I always come back to teaching this course because I enjoy teaching it so much. I feel more rewarded helping these students because as Terry Dean (1989) and Shaughnessy (1977) suggest, these students are more eager to learn, to understand what they need to do to be successful not for this course but for college in general. However, these students, in general, are also more fearful about failing this course than any other. As Connie and Letty demonstrate even after completing the Basic Writing course, many Latino students continue to fear and be frustrated and suspicious about writing and English courses and the instructors who teach these courses. And as my own story shows (see Chapter 1), I relate the complex pedagogical and cultural reasons for my own questions, and I discuss the process that allowed me to succeed when many other Latinos who have struggled with writing do not. I share many of the same suspicions many Latinos have about writing. I have many of the same fears many other Latino students have about writing. I have gone through, and still struggle with issues of identity, resistance, and conflict. I believe this allows me to grasp the concept that the problems Latino students have with writing have less to do with grammar and punctuation and more to do with language, family, and the culture of the students and with how these cultures differ from that of mainstream school.

The goal of this book, as with all studies that deal with communication across cultures, is ultimately to help the student. This book looks at the cultural divide dramatized in the classroom when Latino students attend composition classes taught by Anglo mainstream instructors and examines the communication breakdown that limits learning and performance. The results speak for themselves. Thus, I believe I have argued convincingly for the need to do further research into thus–far–unattended variables in explaining Latino students' frequent failure in Basic Writing courses as well as their high dropout rates. My work also has implications for debate that questions the assumption that education is incremental and that higher–order thinking skills are for those who have mastered elementary knowledge and skills. Clearly, much better thinking is necessary in the area of higher education if we are to address the persistent and pervasive gap in educational attainment of United States–born Latinos. Further work in this area would greatly benefit the field of language and literacy in terms of informing teachers, administrators, and policy makers who are responsible for creating the conditions that will either promote or hinder Latino students' academic achievement.

Although my analysis of these four Latino students does not explain all the reasons for the disproportionately high dropout rates for Latino students, it does give us further insight into why many Latino students reject school, and why many Latino students continue to have problems with writing even after completing their writing classes. As Rosita M.A. Rámirez points out in her ethnographic study, "the educational attainment of Latinos is neither an issue of deficit nor cultural deprivation" (2004). Understanding where students come from and what problems they are having are important when teaching writing because overcoming these problems is key to these students (Latino students) completing college (Valverde, 1987). Understanding the model we use when we teach writing gives us insights into how cultural differences play a part in communication breakdowns between student and teacher (Ybarra, 2001, p. 48).

Similarly, I am always looking for methods that will help make my teaching these students easier. I tried many methods from worksheets to timed writings, but I always come back to the model I am familiar with and that I know works for me: have the students write, then we talk about their writing, then have them rewrite, then we talk about their writing again. Thus, my role as a writing teacher is finding ways to get students to come to class and motivate them to participate. I use my authority to continuously encourage students to talk and to ask questions because I want them to practice speaking (and writing) with authority (Ybarra, 2000). Hence, my role as a writing expert is to actively seek out those students who are having trouble, who are absent from class, who are struggling with writing, and who are in danger of "fading into the woodwork."

Many recent ethnographic studies indicate specifically that there may be different patterns of adaptation in schools, which lead to different school success for immigrant and nonimmigrant minorities, partly because of different historical experiences, which lead to different adaptive responses. As a result, I easily approach writing from different pedagogical and cultural perspectives that provide me with countless opportunities to test, assess, and develop my own ideas about learning and development. Thus, to provide true learning access for all students in the composition classroom, writing/composition instructors must engage in a pedagogy that is inclusive and links cultural differences and approaches to learning objectives as described above. That is to say, the concept of teaching standards and expecting students to perform at that level of standardization implies a learning objective of empowerment. Otherwise the implicit objectives embedded within the notion of standardization of performance cannot be met and many nonmainstream students will continue to fail. Dean (1989) states it this way: "[T]he cultural transitions we ask of our students are by no means easy" (p. 36). And with an enhanced understanding of different cultures, we as educators will better understand the students, which will facilitate the students' transition into the school culture, and us into theirs as well (p. 36).

Composition instructors have the pedagogical responsibility to adapt more inclusive teaching practices in order to provide equal access to learning for all students in their classrooms. To understand how teaching writing affects non–mainstream students (specifically Latinos), we need to understand, describe, and analyze the culture of the classroom using qualitative methods that locate students' attitudes, cultural backgrounds, ethnic patterns of expression and thought, and other cultural information as these students struggle with the demands of the academe (Ybarra, 2001, p.39).

More importantly, if we are to reduce the feelings of alienation, hostility, and anger that many students have with academic writing, particularly Latino students, we need to provide a safe learning environment for all students in the classroom, particularly in composition courses. We, the composition specialists, need to identify the cultural structures embedded in the writing so that we can "adapt to make sure such tropes conscious and use them to help revise our pedagogical assumptions" (Ybarra, 2001, p. 39). These then will help us better create an atmosphere that is conducive to learning for all students, a pedagogy of inclusion, what Lilia Bartolome (1995) has termed "a humanizing pedagogy" (p. 11). This is a pedagogy that takes into account the cultural identities of the students (Ybarra, 2001, p. 169). We must be able to identify student silence as every bit as important as their expressive language. Along these same lines, we must interpret responses (such as "I don't know") in terms of Bartholomae's understanding that such an answer can also be seen as an indication that the student is "not in a position to carry on this discussion"(1988, p. 277).

Notes

1. I cannot speak for Joe because I do not have enough data on him to come up with a conclusion.
2. "Immigrant minority refers not only to those who are actual immigrants but also to those whose ancestors were immigrants and who continue to maintain minority-group identity." Whereas non immigrant minorities refer not only to those who are native born, but to groups incorporated into the host society involuntarily. . .and assigned a subordinate position" (Gibson, 1991, p. 157).

APPENDIX A

Syllabus

UIC Fall 1991	Office Hours:
Instructor	M 11:00–12:00
English 152 82714	2:00–3:00
M,W,F 12:00–12:50	W 2:00–3:00
W 11:00—1:50	F 11:00–12:00

AIMS OF THE COURSE

To develop clarity of thought by reading, thinking, rethinking, redrafting, revising, editing, and polishing prose

To organize and develop ideas in coherent writing

To become confident in writing academic discourse

TEXTS: Bring both texts to every class meeting.

Crossing Cultures: Readings for Composition. Ed. Henry Knepler and Myrna Knepler. New York: Macmillan, 1989.

The Bedford Handbook for Writers. Ed. Diane Hacker. Boston: St. Martin's Press, 1991.

ATTENDANCE AND PARTICIPATION:

It is important that you attend regularly and participate in class activities. Class time will involve instruction, discussion, writing workshops, and individual assistance. All of these are essential to your growth as a writer. Therefore, more than four absences will be grounds for failure.

READING

All the reading assignments in *Crossing Cultures* must be completed by the *beginning of the week for which they are listed.* Our readings are selected to inform our discussions and writings. We will begin looking at culture and families. We will then continue with the struggle of the human spirit to fit in by conforming, stereotyping, scapegoating, destroying others, and destroying self. Our final segment of readings will deal with the survival of the human spirit. Throughout the semester, in class impromptu writings on your reading assignments will be collected and evaluated.

WRITING
In addition to various short in class and homework assignment, there will be six graded writings. Five of these must be typed double spaced, with one inch margins. The sixth writing will be a final in–class essay. At announced times I will ask you to turn in all previous drafts with your final paper. Late papers lose one letter grade for each class meeting they are late.

GRADING
Attendance and participation in class are prerequisites for passing. The final grade for the course will be based on the six graded writings (90%) and in class writing (10%).

PROPOSED SYLLABUS:

Week 1—Read "Customs" (247–251) and "American Men Don't Cry" (209–292).

Week 2—Read "Families" (85–89) and "Fitting In" (123–127).
No class on Monday, Sept. 2.

Week 3—Read "Girlhood among Ghosts" (15–20) and "Halfway to Dick and Jane" (21–33).

Week 4—Read "Hair" (120–122), "Shooting an Elephant" (228–235), and "The Village of Ben Suc" (209–215).

Week 5—Writing #1 due.

Week 6—Read "Custer Died for Your Sins" (331–334) and "Incident" (37).

Week 7—Read "When I Was a Child" (47–54).

Week 8—Read "From Vietnam, 1979" (165–169).

Week 9—Read "Arrival at Manzanar" (158–164).

Week 10—Read "We Real Cool" (136).

Week 11—Writings #3 and #4 due.

Week 12—Read "Graduation" (3–14) and "Alien Turf" (145–157).

Week 13—Read "I Learn What I Am" (139–144).

Week 14—Writing #5 due. No Class Friday, Nov. 29.

Week 15—Writing #6: in class essay.

APPENDIX B

Worksheet Exercises

APPOSITIVES: Remake the following sentences into one sentence by using an appositive.

1. During Lent of 1968 César Chávez began his twenty five–day fast. César Chávez is the hero of California's farmworkers.

2. Maya Angelou speaks simply and profoundly of her life story in *I Know Why the Cage Bird Sings*. Maya is a renowned author, singer and actress.

3. In 1955 Rosa Parks changed the world when she boarded the Cleveland Avenue bus in downtown Montgomery. Rosa Parks was a seamstress employed by a local department store.

4. Rosa was returning home after her regular day's work in the Montgomery Fair. Montgomery Fair is a leading department store in downtown Montgomery.

5. The race car belonging to Janet Guthrie was stolen on Saturday. Janet was a driver at the Indianapolis 500.

6. Soccer is gaining fans in the United States. It is the most popular sport in the world.

7. *Roots* is the story of seven generations of one man's family. The book is an invaluable contribution to American history.

8. The Mayan kingdom covered most of Central America. The Mayan kingdom was a loose federation of cities.

9. Florida alligators have made a comeback from near extinction to a population of more than a million. Florida alligators are animals protected from hunters since 1962.

10. In 1984 Northrop turned over $6.25 million to a company that was not a usual supplier. Northrop is a Los Angeles–based defense contractor.
11. Steve Jobs is a co founder of Apple Computer and one of the world's

most famous entrepreneurs. News raced through Silicon Valley that Steve Jobs was ready to announce a new computer.

PREPOSITIONAL PHRASES

1. One of the interesting things about human beings is that they try to understand themselves and their own behavior.

2. Many insights into human behavior are gained by understanding a people's design for living.

3. To the American woman a system of multiple wives seems instinctively abhorrent.

4. The details of his physical appearance were more important than the movement of his gestures.

5. The incest taboos between members of the same class are as severe as those between true brothers and sisters.

6. The shame of the Indians at the suggestion that a clan brother and sister should dance together represents a cultural response to a differing cultural situation.

7. The files of the Cross Cultural Survey at the Yale University are organized according to categories such as "marriage ceremonies," "life crisis rites," and "incest taboos."

8. The biological potentialities of a person are the building blocks of culture.

9. The facts of nature limit cultural forms.

10. The return of the disequilibrated organ systems of the body to steady states or dynamic stability is known as homeostasis.

11. Any interference with the homeostatic mechanisms is likely to be damaging to the organism.

12. The counter magic of the witch doctors is unusual in its lack of ritual. The memory displayed by the Nacirema in these exorcism sessions is truly remarkable.

13. Our review of the ritual life of the Nacirema people has shown them to

be a people grounded in the security of ritual.

14. The sacred and traditional character of these rites is evident in the fact the natives return to the holy–mouth men year after year.

15. Few applicants in the temple are well enough to do anything but lie on their hard beds.

16. Among cultures of the West, the number of nonsexual uses of the kiss is staggering.

APPENDIX C

Connie's Essay

When two cultures collide is the time when true suffering exists.
—Hermann Hesse

I find this quote to be true in my case. Although my parents are from Ecuador and Argentina, I was born here in the United States. Their culture is very different from the American culture. The values that my parents have are considered "old fashion" to American values and to my own.

In my parents' culture there are certain ways a girl should act and another way a guy should act. Girls cannot stay out late, have boyfriends until a certain age, or if they do have a boyfriend they cannot engage in any sexual behavior. Guys, however, can stay out late, have girlfriends at any age, and have sexual relationships because it's their nature to. I think my parents' culture is made up of values that are double standards.

In America's culture, equality is considered one of the most important parts in being an American. Although in some places equality is denied to some, Americans have the right to fight it. There are not as many double standards as in my parents' cultural values.

My parents' values are old fashioned. For example, they think it's wrong to kiss my boyfriend in public. It's wrong to have my boyfriend come over when I'm home by myself. My parents enforce these values because they worry about what people might think. They're afraid people will see them as bad and uncaring parents. I don't believe that bringing my boyfriend to my house when I'm by myself is a sign of not caring or showing disrespect to my parents. It is acceptable for me to do this because it's part of other values I have, the American values.

American values have taught me to be independent. We as Americans have a right to speak up on things we don't agree on. That is why I always rebelled against my parents' cultural rules. In American culture with another culture I'm deprived of some of my freedom. Freedom that is automatically given to anyone who is born in the United States. The little freedom that I did have helped me find my values.

My values are influenced by both cultures. Although I do not agree a hundred percent with my parents' values, I feel they're good and morally right to some extent. Finding values that are important to me separates me from others and makes me an individual.

All these different values have caused me to struggle in finding out who I am and what I stand for. It was frustrating growing up with two different and virtually opposite cultures. When I get older, maybe I'll appreciate the different cultural values and teach them to my children with an open mind.

APPENDIX D

Letty's Essay

We all need to belong to something, something that can give us meaning in life. The meaning we find in life is largely determined by culture. Culture has influenced expectations that stem from many people in my life. My cultural expectations were and still are influenced by my family, my cultural background, and my peers.

In my family, education is highly stressed. Their expectations put a great amount of pressure on me. At times, it seems that they want me to accomplish what they didn't. They just want what they think is best for me. For example my father wants me to study hard and succeed in life, and not have it as rough as he did. When I was younger it was much easier I was the one who pushed myself. Now, they are the ones that motivate me and I don't want to disappoint them. I am striving because of their support and confidence in me. Because of their support and confidence in me, I am striving to be the first in my family to graduate from college.

My cultural background has caused some difficulties in my life. My parents are not from this country. They were both born in Mexico as were my four brothers and two sisters. I was the only one born in the United States. I grew up with my parents' values and ideas, as well as American values. My parents are still struggling with trying to adapt to the new way of life because they still hold on to their old–fashioned way of thinking. Then came the conflict between my parents and my peers. Now, the influences that came from my peers changed a lot of the intentions that my parents hoped I had and kept. My peers have been an important facet in my life. It wasn't until not too long ago that I realized that my parents and I have many things in common. They often have the same cultural background and their families' expectations of them were the same as mine. We found that we had the same values that our parents had implied, but yet we were coming up with our own way of thinking. Because of them, I was encouraged to be more of my own person. I had to combine these different aspects and try to make them fit together as best as I could. To this day, it is still hard to make sense meet, but as time passes it is getting easier. As Hermann Hesse stated, "When two cultures collide is the only time when true suffering exists."

I have grown from these expectations and values set by my family. I have my own ideas, but yet I still hold those that my parents taught me. Like every person I want to be happy and successful in life. I want to feel comfortable with the values that I have set for myself, whether they have been handed down to me or whether I have created them myself. Without culture, I wouldn't be who and what I am. All things in life have helped me and have been the building blocks of my life. The chain will continue for generations to come. Not everyone's cultural expectations will be the same, but they will have a little of the culture that has come from many generations ago. Thomas Carlyle once said, "The great law of culture: let each become all that he has created capable of being."

BIBLIOGRAPHY

Ávila, Margis Bertha. (2002). Xicanas(os) *Claming Authentic Voice: The Process of Conscientization Xicanas(os) Experience in Claiming Authentic Voice.* Paper presented at the 2002 Annual Meeting of the American Educational Research Association, New Orleans.

Bartholomae, David. (1988a). Inventing the University. In Eugene R. Kintgen, Barry M. Kroll, and M. Rose (Eds.), *Perspectives on Literacy* (pp. 273–285). Carbondale: Southern Illinois University Press.

———. (1988b). The Study of Error. In G. Tate and E. Corbett (Eds.), *The Writing Teacher's Sourcebook* 2nd edition (pp. 303–317). New York: Oxford University Press.

Bartolome, Lilia. (October, 1995). *A Humanizing Pedagogy: Collapsing Cultural and Disciplinary Boundaries.* Paper Presentated at the University of Massachusetts, Boston,

Bizzell, Patricia. (1986). Beyond Anti Foundationalism in Compositions Studies. *Pre/Text*, 7.1–7.2, pp. 37–56.

-Bloome, David. (1989). Introduction. In David Bloome (Ed.), *Classrooms and Literacy* (pp. 1–28). Norwood, NJ: Ablex.

Bonvillain, Nancy. (1993). *Language, Culture, and Communication: The Meaning of Messages.* Englewood Cliffs, NJ: Prentice–Hall.

Cazden, Courtney. (1986). Classroom Discourse. In M. C. Wittrock (Ed.), *Handbook of Research on Teaching* (pp. 432–463). New York: Macmillan.

D'Amato, John. (1993). Resistance and Compliance in Minority Classrooms. In Evelyn Jacob and Cathie Jordan (Eds.), *Minority Education: Anthropological Perspectives* (pp. 181–207). Norwood, NJ: Ablex.

Dean, Terry. (1989). Multicultural Classroom, Monocultural Teachers. *College Composition and Communication,* 40(1), pp.1–23

Downs, Nancy et al. (1991). *A Syllabus for English 152.* Chicago: University of Illinois at Chicago, Department of English.

Eisenhart, Margaret and Elizabeth Graue. (1993). Constructing Cultural Differences and Educational Achievement in Schools. In Evelyn Jacob and Cathie Jordan (Eds.), *Minority Education: Anthropological Perspectives* (pp. 165–179). Norwood, NJ: Ablex.

Elbow, Peter. (1991). Reflections on Academic Discourse: How It Relates to Freshman and Colleagues. *College English*, 53(2), pp. 135–155.

Erickson, Fedrick. (1996). Transformation and School Success: The Politics and Culture of Educational Achievement. In Evelyn Jacob and Cathie Jordan (Eds.), *Minority Education: Anthropological Perspectives* (pp. 27–51). Norwood, NJ: Ablex.

Farr, Marcia. (1992). Essayist Literacy and Other Verbal Performances. *Written Communication,* 10(1), pp. 4–38.

———. (1991). Biliteracy in the Home: Practices among Mexicano Families in Chicago. Paper prepared for Biliteracy Colloquia Center for Applied Linguistics, Washington, DC.

———. (1990). *Oral Texts and Literacy among Mexican Immigrants in Chicago.* Chicago: Spencer Foundation

———. (1986). Language Culture, and Writing: Sociolinguistic Foundations of Research Writing. In E. Rothkopf (Ed.), *Review of Research in Education* (pp. 195–221). Washington, DC: American Education Research Association.

Farr, Marcia, and Harvey Daniels. (1986). *Language Diversity and Writing Instruction.* New York: ERIC Clearinghouse on Urban Education Institute for Urban and Minority Education.

Fraher, Richard. (1984). Learning a New Art: Suggestions for Beginning Teachers. In Morganroth Gullette (Ed.), *The Art and Craft of Teaching* (pp. 116–127). Cambridge, MA: Harvard University Press.

Friere, Paulo. (1997). *Pedagogy of the Oppressed* 20th edition. Myra Bergman Ramos (trans). New York: Continuum.

Gibson, Margaret. (1996). The School Performance of Immigrant Minorities: A Comparative View. In Evelyn Jacob and Cathie Jordan (Eds.), *Minority Education: Anthropological Perspectives* (pp. 113–128). Norwood, NJ: Ablex.

Gibson, Margaret. (1991). *Minority Status and Schooling: A Comparative Study of Immigrant and Involuntary Minorities.* New York: Garland.

Giroux, Henry A. (1992). *Border Crossings: Cultural Workers and the Politics of Education.* New York: Routledge.

Gonzalez, Gabriela. (2004). The Effects of Family Background, Immigration Status and Social Context on Latino Children's Educational Attainment. In Raul Ybarra and Nancy López (Eds.) *Creating Alternative Discourses in the Education of Latinos and Latinas: A Reader.* New York: Peter Lang.

Gumperz, Jenny Cook and John J. Gumperz. (1982). Introduction: Language and the Communication of Social Identify. In John Gumperz (Ed.),

Language and Social Identity (pp. 1–21). Cambridge, U.K.: Cambridge University Press.

Gumperz, John J. (1982). *Discourse Strategies: Studies in Interactional Sociolinguistics 1*. New York: Cambridge University Press.

Hacker, Diane. (1991). *The Bedford Handbook for Writers* 3rd edition. Boston: Bedford Books.

Harris, Joseph. (1989). The Idea of Community in the Study of Writing. *College, Composition and Communication*, 40(1), pp. 11–22.

Hartwell, Patrick. (1985). Grammar, Grammars, and the Teaching of Grammar. *College English*, 47, pp. 105–127.

Haswell, Richard. (1988). Dark Shadows: The Fate of Writers at the Bottom. *College, Composition and Communication*, 39(3), pp. 303–315.

Heath, Shirley B. (1983). *Ways with Words: Language, Life and Working Communities and Classrooms*. Cambridge, MA: Cambridge University Press.

———. (1982). Ethnography in Education: Defining the Essentials. In Perry Gilmore and Allan A. Glatthorn (Eds.), *Children In and Out of School: Ethnography in Education* (pp.33–55). Washington DC: Center for Applied Linguistics.

———. (1978). *Teacher Talk: Language in the Classroom*. Language in Education: Theory and Practice 9. Arlington VA: Center for Applied Linguistics.

hooks, bell. (1994). *Teaching to Transgress: Education as the Practice of Freedom*. New York: Routledge.

Hymes, Dell. (1974). *Foundations in Sociolinguistics: An Ethnographic Approach*. Philadelphia: University of Pennsylvania Press.

Jacob, Evelyn and Cathie Jordan. (1996). Understanding Minority Education: Framing the Issues. In Evelyn Jacob and Cathie Jordan (Eds.), *Minority Education: Anthropological Perspectives* (pp. 3–15). Norwood, NJ: Ablex.

Jepp, T. C. et al. (1993). Language and Disadvantage: The Hidden Process. In John Gumperz (Ed.), *Language and Social Identity* (pp. 1–21). Cambridge, U.K.: Cambridge University Press.

Knopp, Linda. (1995). Remedial Education: An Undergraduate Student Profile. *Research Briefs, The American Council on Education, Division of Policy and Research*, 6(8), pp. 1–11.

Kutz, Eleanor, Suzy Q. Groden, and, Vivian Zamel. (1993). *The Discovery of Competence: Teaching and Learning with Diverse Student Writers*. Portsmouth, NH: Boynton/Cook.

Kutz, Eleanor and Hephzibah Roskelly. (1991). *An Unquiet Pedagogy: Transforming Practice in the English Classroom*. Portsmouth, NH: Boynton/Cook.

López, Nancy. (2004). Rewriting Race and Gender High School Lessons: Second Generation Dominicans in New York City. In Raul Ybarra and Nancy López (Eds.), *Creating Alternative Discourses in the Education of Latinos and Latinas: A Reader*. New York: Peter Lang.

Mehan, Hugh. (1979). *Learning Lessons*. Cambridge, MA: Harvard University Press.

Mirón, Louis F. (1997). *Resisting Discrimination: Affirmative Strategies for Principals and Teachers*. Thousand Oaks, CA: Corwin Press.

Moll, Luis. (1988). Key Issues in Teaching Latino Students. *Language Arts* 65, pp. 465- 472.

Ogbu, John. (1996). Framework—Variability in Minority School Performance: A Problem in Search of an Explanation. In Evelyn Jacobs and Cathie Jordan (Eds.), *Minority Education: Anthropological Perspective* (pp. 83–111). Norwood, NJ: Ablex.

———. (1993). Literacy and Schooling in Subordinate Cultures: The Case of Black Americans. In Eugene R. Kintgen, Barry M. Kroll, and Mike Rose (Eds.), *Perspectives on Literacy* (pp. 227–242). Carbondale: Southern Illinois University Press.

———. (1991). Immigrant and Involuntary Minorities in Comparative Perspective. In John Ogbu and Margaret Gibson's (Eds.), *Minority Status and Schooling: A Comparative Study of Immigrant and Involuntary Minorities* (pp. 3–33). New York: Garland.

———. (Spring 1990). Minority Status and Literacy in Comparative Perspective. *Daedalus*, 119(2), pp. 141–165.

———. (1987). Opportunity Structure, Cultural Boundaries, and Literacy. In Judith Langer (Ed.), *Literacy and Culture: Issues of Society and Schooling* (pp. 149–177). Norwood, NJ: Ablex.

Padilla, Raymond V. and Rudolfo Chávez Chávez. (1993). Introduction. In Raymond V Padilla and Rudolfo Chávez Chávez (Eds.), *The Leaning Ivory Tower: Latino Professors in American Universities* (pp. 1–16). Albany: State University of New York Press.

Pascarella, E.T. (Winter 1980). Student–Faculty Informal Contact and College Outcomes. *Review of Educational Research*, 50(4), pp. 545–595.

Philips, Susan. (1983). *The Invisible Culture: Communication in the Classroom and Community on the Warm Springs Indian Reservation.* Prospect Heights, IL: Waveland Press.

Porter, Oscar F. (1990). *Undergraduate Completion and Persistence at Four Year Colleges and Universities: Detailed Findings.* Washington DC: National Institute of Independent Colleges and Universities (NIICU).

Rámirez, M. A. Rosita. (2004). Latino Parents Put into Words: Immigrant Parents Share Their Beliefs on Education through an After–School Parents, Children and Computers Project. In Raul Ybarra and Nancy López (eds.) *Creating Alternative Discourses in the Education of Latinos and Latinas*: A Reader, New York: Peter Lang.

Randell, D. R. (1998). The Logic of Indirection: The Polychronic Mode and Other Stories. Unpublished paper.

Rivera, Lorna. (October 2001). Can Adult Education Programs Provide a Way Out? A Study of Popular Education and Homeless Mothers. Paper presented at the Trapped by Poverty/Trapped by Abuse Research Conference, University of Michigan, Ann Arbor.

Rose, Mike. (1989). *Lives on the Boundary.* New York: Penguin.

———. (October 1988a). Narrowing the Mind and Page: Remedial Writers and Cognitive Reductionism. *College Composition and Communication*, 39(3), pp. 267–302.

———. (1988b). Remedial Writing Courses: A Critique and a Proposal. In G. Tate and E. Corbett (Eds.), *The Writing Teacher's Sourcebook* (pp. 318–337). New York: Oxford University Press.

Russell, Bertrand. (1967). *The Autobiography of Bertrand Russell 1972–1914.* London: Allen and Unwin.

Saville Troike, Muriel. (1989). *The Ethnography of Communication,* 2nd edition. New York: Basil Blackwell.

Scollon, R. and S. B. Scollon. (1981). *Narrative, Literacy and Face in Interethnic Communication.* Norwood, NJ: Ablex.

Shaughnessy, Mina. (1977). *Errors and Expectations: A Guide for the Teacher of Basic Writing.* New York: Oxford University Press.

Soto, Lourdes Diaz. (1997). *Language, Culture and Power: Bilingual Families and the Struggle for Quality Education.* Albany: State University of New York Press.

Staton Ann Q. (1990). *Communication and Student Socialization*. Norwood, NJ: Ablex.

Stock, Patricia and Jay Robinson. (1989). Literacy as Conversation: Classroom Talk as Text Building. In David Bloome (Ed.), *Classrooms and Literacy* (pp. 310–411). Norwood, NJ: Ablex.

Stubbs, Michael. (1983). *Discourse Analysis: The Sociolinguistic Analysis of Natural Language*. Chicago: University of Chicago Press.

Tinto, Vincent. (1987). *Leaving College: Rethinking the Causes and Cures of Student Attrition* 2nd edition. Chicag: University of Chicago Press.

U. S. Department of Education. (1992). National Center for Educational Statistics 1992. (NCES Publication 92697). Washington, DC: U. S. Printing Government Office.

U. S. Department of Education. (1993). Digest of Education Statistics 1993 (NCES Publication 93292). Washington, DC: U. S. Government Printing Office.

University of Illinois at Chicago (UIC). (February 1994). *UIC Student Data Book for 1989–93*. Chicago: University of Illinois at Chicago, Data Resources and Institutional Analysis.

Valenzuela, Angela. (1999). *Subtractive Schooling: U.S.–Mexican Youth and the Politics: The Politics of Caring*. Albany: State University of New York Press.

Valverde, Sylvia A. (1987). A Comparative Study of Hispanics High School Dropouts and Graduates. *Education and Urban Society*, 19(3), pp. 320–329.

Walsh, Catherine E. (1991). *Pedagogy and the Struggle for Voice: Issues of Language, Power, and Schooling for Puerto Ricans*. Westport, CT: Bergin Garvy.

Watkins, Floyd C. and, William B. Dillingham (1989). *The Practical English Handbook*. Boston: Houghton Mifflin.

Ybarra, Raul. (2001). Cultural Dissonance in Basic Writing Courses. *Journal of Basic Writing* 20(1), pp. 37–52.

———. (Fall 2000) Latino Students and Anglo Mainstream Instructors: An Ethnographic Study of Classroom Communication. *Journal of College Student Retention: Research, Theory & Practice* 2(2), pp. 161–171.

———. (1992). Western Essayist Literacy: A Way of Teaching (ERIC Document Reproduction Service NO. ED. 346489).

INDEX

A

B

C

D

E

F

G

H

I

J

K

L

M

O

P

R

S

T

U

V

W

Y

Z

COUNTERPOINTS

Studies in the Postmodern Theory of Education

General Editors
Joe L. Kincheloe & Shirley R. Steinberg

Counterpoints publishes the most compelling and imaginative books being written in education today. Grounded on the theoretical advances in criticalism, feminism, and postmodernism in the last two decades of the twentieth century, Counterpoints engages the meaning of these innovations in various forms of educational expression. Committed to the proposition that theoretical literature should be accessible to a variety of audiences, the series insists that its authors avoid esoteric and jargonistic languages that transform educational scholarship into an elite discourse for the initiated. Scholarly work matters only to the degree it affects consciousness and practice at multiple sites. Counterpoints' editorial policy is based on these principles and the ability of scholars to break new ground, to open new conversations, to go where educators have never gone before.

For additional information about this series or for the submission of manuscripts, please contact:

Joe L. Kincheloe & Shirley R. Steinberg
c/o Peter Lang Publishing, Inc.
275 Seventh Avenue, 28th floor
New York, New York 10001

To order other books in this series, please contact our Customer Service Department:

Or browse online by series: